SURVEY RESEARCH METHODS

Applied Social Research Methods Series
Volume 1

Applied Social Research Methods Series

Series Editor:
LEONARD BICKMAN, Peabody College, Vanderbilt University

Series Associate Editor:
DEBRA ROG, Joint Legislative Audit and
Review Commission, Commonwealth of Virginia

This series is designed to provide students and practicing professionals in the social sciences with relatively inexpensive softcover textbooks describing the major methods used in applied social research. Each text introduces the reader to the state of the art of that particular method and follows step-by-step procedures in its explanation. Each author describes the theory underlying the method to help the student understand the reasons for undertaking certain tasks. Current research is used to support the author's approach. Examples of utilization in a variety of applied fields, as well as sample exercises, are included in the books to aid in classroom use.

Volumes in this series:

Additional volumes currently in development

SURVEY RESEARCH METHODS

Floyd J. Fowler, Jr.

Applied Social Research Methods Series
Volume 1

 SAGE PUBLICATIONS Beverly Hills London New Delhi

For information address:

SAGE Publications, Inc.
275 South Beverly Drive
Beverly Hills, California 90212

SAGE Publications India Pvt. Ltd.
C-236 Defence Colony
New Delhi 110 024, India

SAGE Publications Ltd
28 Banner Street
London EC1Y 8QE, England

Printed in the United States of America

Library of Congress Cataloging in Publication Data

Fowler, Floyd J.
  Survey research methods.

  (Applied social research methods texts ; v. 1)
  1. Social surveys. I. Title. II. Series.
HN29.F68   1984   301′.0723   84-9862
ISBN 0-8039-2347-3
ISBN 0-8039-2348-1 (pbk.)

FIFTH PRINTING, 1987

CONTENTS

PREFACE

For nearly 20 years, I have wished for a book like this one. I have spent class time lecturing that could have been spent better discussing applications and implications if students had read a good overview of survey research issues. Nonresearchers have come to the Center for Survey Research thinking they wanted to do a survey; they needed to gain an understanding of the various steps involved in a survey, the decisions to be made, and their significance. Colleagues who were not methodologists have expressed a need for a detailed presentation of survey research issues to which they should attend.

Heretofore, I have not had a book to give to such people. I am grateful to Len Bickman, the editor of this series, and to Sage for giving me the occasion and impetus for writing it.

Certainly the hardest part of writing the book was keeping it short. That meant a lot of choices about the amount of detail provided on various topics. The brevity of the book will, however, provide an appropriate level of detail for many readers, and a good basis from which to delve into more specialized sources for others.

I want to acknowledge intellectual debts to Charles Cannell, Morris Axelrod, Robert Kahn, and Angus Campbell, each of whom helped to teach me in different ways and areas how the details of the research process matter and to convince me that trying to make each aspect of each data collection better was a worthy task to which to be committed.

Debra Rog provided helpful editing. Marcia McCollin and Anstis Benfield did most of the typing. Many colleagues kindly reviewed drafts. The Center for Survey Research let me have time and support services for this task. Judy Chambliss played a critical role in the maintenance of the mental health that the effort required. Of course, the responsibility for what is herein, good and bad, is basically mine.

Boston, Massachusetts   *—Jack Fowler*

1

Introduction

This book is about standards and practical procedures for surveys designed to provide statistical descriptions of people by asking questions, usually of a sample. Surveys meld sampling, question design, and interviewing methodologies. Those who want to collect, analyze, or read about survey data will learn how details of each aspect of a survey can affect its precision, accuracy, and credibility.

The subject of this book is data collection in social surveys. It includes common procedures, standards for good practice, and the implications of various design decisions for the quality of survey data. The purpose of the book is to give a sound basis for evaluating data collection procedures to those who would collect, analyze, or read about survey data. Readers will come to understand the ways in which the details of data collection are related to the confidence they can have in figures and statistics based on surveys.

There are many data collection and measurement processes that are called surveys. This book focuses on those surveys that have the following characteristics:

(1) The purpose of the survey is to produce statistics—that is, quantitative or numerical descriptions of some aspects of the study population.
(2) The main way of collecting information is by asking people questions; their answers constitute the data to be analyzed.
(3) Generally, information is collected about only a fraction of the population—that is, a sample—rather than from every member of the population.

REASONS FOR SURVEYS

In the United States Constitution it is specified that a survey meeting the above criteria must be carried out every ten years, the Decennial Census: Statistics are produced about a population by asking people questions. In the Census, however, no sampling is involved; data are collected from *every* household in the population.

The purpose of the Decennial Census is to count people as a basis for ensuring appropriate representation in the House of Representatives. However, the Census also has become a major source of information for many other purposes because, in addition to simple counts, it collects data about the race, age, household composition, education, type of housing, and many other characteristics of the people counted.

The content of the Decennial Census has expanded increasingly to meet the needs of government agencies and researchers for descriptive data. However, the content covers only a small portion of what people want to know about populations, and its value is limited because it occurs only once per decade. To provide data to fill those information gaps, special-purpose surveys have become a prevalant part of American life since the 1930s.

Most people are familiar with three uses of survey techniques: the measurement of public opinion for newspaper and magazine articles, the measurement of political perceptions and opinions to help political candidates with their elections, and market research designed to understand better consumer preferences and interests. Each of these well-developed programs of survey research is aimed primarily at tapping the subjective feelings of the public.

There is, in addition, a wide variety of applications of survey research methodology that focuses on factual material (i.e., people's behavior or situations). Numerous facts about our population can be obtained only by asking a sample of people about themselves. In fact, there probably is no area of public policy to which survey research methodology has not been applied. The following is an abbreviated list of some of the major applications:

(1) Unemployment rates, as released routinely by the Bureau of Labor Statistics, as well as many other statistics about jobs and work, are based on surveys carried out by the Bureau of the Census. Parallel surveys of businesses and industries are carried out to describe production and manpower needs.

(2) People's incomes and the way they spend their money constitute another area in which only surveys can provide reliable data. Patterns of consumer expenditures and their expectations have proven to be important predictors of trends in the economy.

(3) The National Health Interview Survey has been carried out by the Bureau of the Census for the Public Health Service since the late 1950s. This survey collects basic data about health conditions, use of health services, and health care expenditures. These are all

topics about which only good survey research can provide adequate data.

(4) The main source of data about criminal events traditionally has come from police departmemt records. However, police records only include events that people report to police. For most crimes involving victims, surveys provide a more reliable measure of the rate at which crimes occur and the way in which they are distributed. Hence the National Crime Survey was launched in the 1970s to provide those figures. In addition, surveys are the only way to measure people's concerns and fears about crime.

(5) One of the oldest applications of surveys is by the U.S. Department of Agriculture. The Department surveys farmers to estimate the rate at which different crops will be planted and to predict the availability of various food products.

Mental health, transportation needs and patterns of use, political behavior, characteristics of housing, its cost and appropriateness to family needs, and worker satisfaction are other examples of areas where survey research is used extensively.

The largest collector of survey data in the United States is undoubtedly the federal government—particularly the Bureau of the Census and the Department of Agriculture. However, universities and nonprofit and for-profit survey organizations exist and are active throughout the United States and elsewhere.

Sponsoring a special-purpose survey data collection is a rather expensive solution to an information problem. Before someone launches such an effort, one should explore thoroughly the potential for gathering the same information from existing records or from other sources. Unfortunately, some people think of a survey as a first effort to try to learn something about a population; more appropriately, a full-scale probability survey should be undertaken only after it is certain that the information cannot be obtained in other ways and the need for information is significant. Even taking such a conservative approach, it is common to find that only a special-purpose survey can provide a needed estimate of how things are in a population.

There are four reasons for deciding to do a survey:

(1) *Probability sampling* enables one to have confidence that the sample is not a biased one and to estimate how precise the data are likely to be. Data from a properly chosen sample are a great improvement over data from a sample of those who attend meetings, speak loudest, volunteer to respond, or happen to be convenient to poll.

(2) *Standardized measurement* that is consistent across all respondents ensures that one has comparable information about ev-

eryone involved in the survey. Without such measurement, analyzing distributions or patterns of association is not meaningful.

(3) As noted above, although record data can be used for some research purposes, a main reason for surveys is to *collect information that is available from no other source*.

(4) *Analysis requirements* may dictate a special-purpose survey. Even if there is information about some set of events, it may not be paired with other characteristics needed to carry out a desired analysis. For example, hospital discharge records invariably lack information about income. Hence a survey that collects income and hospitalization data about people is needed in order to study the relationship between a person's income and hospitalization experience.

There is always some information available on a given topic from what people say, from impressions, or from records. Whether or not additional information is worth the cost of a survey depends on the situation. The strengths of survey methods, however, that result in their wide use are the value of statistical sampling, consistent measurement, and the ability to obtain information not systematically available elsewhere or in the form needed for analyses.

THE COMPONENTS OF SURVEYS

Like all measures in all sciences, social survey measurement is not error free. The procedures used to conduct a survey have a major effect on the likelihood the resulting data will describe accurately what is intended to be described.

A sample survey brings together three different methodological areas: sampling, designing questions, and interviewing. Each of these techniques has many applications outside of sample surveys, but their combination is essential to good survey design.

Sampling

A census means gaining information about every individual in a population. A major development in the process of making surveys useful was learning how to sample, to select a small subset of a population representative of the whole population. The key to good sampling is finding a way to give all (or nearly all) population members the same (or a known) chance of being sampled, and to use probability methods for choosing the sample.

Early surveys and polls often relied on samples of convenience or on sampling from lists that excluded significant portions of the population. These did not provide reliable, credible figures.

The Department of Agriculture actually developed the procedures for drawing the comprehensive probability samples needed to provide statistically reliable descriptions of populations living in a definable area. The procedures evolved from work designed to sample land areas for predicting crop yields. Sampling housing units and the people living in those housing units was simply an extension of that work.

During World War II, a group of social scientists was housed in the Department of Agriculture to do social surveys related to the war effort. It was then that area probability sampling became firmly entrenched for sampling general populations in social surveys. Area probability sampling is still the method of choice for personal interview surveys.

Strategies for sampling have been refined since 1950. The most notable advance has been the development of random digit dialing to sample households with telephones. However, the principles of good sampling practice have been well developed for a long time.

Question Design

Using questions as measures is another essential part of the survey process. The initial survey efforts, representing extensions of journalism, were not careful about the way that questions were posed. It soon became apparent, however, that sending an interviewer out with a set of question objectives without providing specific question wording produced important differences in the answers that were obtained. Thus early in the 20th century, researchers began to write standardized questions for measuring subjective phenomena. In the 1940s, researchers at the U.S. Department of Agriculture again are given credit for extending the use of standardized questions to situations in which factual or objective information was sought.

Payne (1951) published a landmark book providing practical guidelines for researchers for writing clear questions that interviewers could administer as worded and respondents could answer without amplification. Likert (1932) generally is credited for building a bridge between the elaborate scaling techniques developed by psychophysical psychologists for measuring subjective phenomena (e.g., Thurstone, 1929) and the practical requirements of applied social survey research. Although there has been considerable progress since Likert's early work to develop batteries of questions that best measure specific events and phenomena, the principles of standardized question design have been largely unamended since the early 1950s.

Interviewing

Although all surveys do not involve interviewing, as some surveys have respondents answer self-administered questions, it certainly is common to use an interviewer to ask questions and record answers. When interviewers are used, it is important to avoid having them influence the answers respondent give, at the same time maximizing the accuracy with which questions are answered.

The first major step in increasing interviewer consistency was to give them standardized questions. It subsequently was found that interviewers also needed to be trained in how to administer a survey in order to avoid introducing important biases in the answers they obtained (Friedman, 1942). Hyman et al. (1954) published a series of studies documenting ways other than question wording that interviewers could influence the answers they obtained. His work led to more elaborate training of interviewers with respect to strategies for probing when incomplete answers are obtained and for handling the interpersonal aspects of the interview in nonbiasing ways. Cannell and his associates (1977b) have moved further along the process of trying to reduce between-interviewer variation by specifically scripting the introductions and encouragement that interviewers provide to respondents, while limiting unstructured discussion.

Research on how to improve interviewing continues. However, principles for achieving standardization and minimizing bias caused by interviewers have not changed much since the 1950s; the main thrust of more recent work has been the development of procedures, training, and supervision programs to improve interviewer execution of those principles.

Total Survey Design

Thus in major ways, the principles for good research practice were well developed in the United States by the early 1950s. However, an important fact about the practice of survey research in the United States is that many of the principles well established in the 1950s are not routinely a part of many social surveys. Bailar and Lanphier (1978) and Turner and Martin (1984) provide examples of relatively poor practice in the collection of survey data.

There are many reasons for variation in the quality of surveys. For some surveys, imprecise figures will suffice. Lack of funding and lack of adequate staff as well as lack of methodological knowledge no doubt all contribute to poor practice in some cases. However, one feature of survey research design that is partly to blame is the failure of researchers to put together good quality procedures in all three of the salient areas; it is not uncommon to see researchers attend carefully to some aspects of good survey design at the same time they neglect others. A critical orientation of this book is the so-called total survey design perspective.

Every survey involves a number of decisions that have the potential to enhance or detract from the accuracy (or precision) of survey estimates. Generally, the decisions that would lead one to have "better" data involve more money, time, or other resources. Thus the design of a survey involves a set of decisions to optimize the use of resources. Optimal design will take into account all the salient aspects of the survey process.

With respect to sampling, critical issues include the following:

(1) The choice of whether or not to use a probability sample.
(2) The sample frame, or those people who actually have a chance to be sampled.
(3) The size of the sample.
(4) The sample design, or the particular strategy used for sampling people or households.
(5) The rate of response, or the percentage of those sampled for whom data are actually collected.

With respect to questionnaire design, the researcher must decide the extent to which previous literature regarding the reliability and validity of questions is drawn upon, the use made of consultants who are experts in question design, and the investment to be made in pretesting and pilot work.

With respect to interviewers, researchers have choices to make about the amount and kind of training and supervision to give.

A design decision cutting across all these areas is *the mode of data collection,* whether the researcher will collect data by telephone, by mail, by personal interview, or in some other way. That decision has important cost implications and affects the quality of data that will be collected.

These pieces taken together constitute what is called the total survey design. The components of the design are interrelated in two important ways. First, the quality of data will be no better than the most error-prone feature of the survey design. In the past, researchers sometimes have focused on one or two features of the survey, such as the size of the sample or the response rate, to evaluate the likely quality of data. However, current best practice requires examination of *all* of the above design features. If there is a major compromise or weakness in any aspect of the survey design, major investments in other portions of the survey are not sensible. For example, if one is asking questions that respondents are unlikely to be able to answer with great precision, a very large sample aimed at reducing sampling error to a minimum is likely to be unwarranted. Similarly, and perhaps even more common, a large number of survey responses will not increase credibility if the sample is poorly designed, or the rate of response is so low as to make the sample unlikely to be representative, or interviewers are trained and supervised poorly.

For designers and users of survey research, the total survey design approach means asking questions about all of these features, not just a few, when attempting to evaluate the quality of a survey and the credibility of a particular data set.

PURPOSES AND GOALS OF TEXT

This text presents a discussion of the major decisions that go into the design of any survey research project, the options available to the researcher, and the potential significance of the various options for the amount of error and the credibility of survey estimates. When appropriate, a set of procedures that would constitute good survey practice is presented. A serious effort is made to discuss the realities and the practical problems with which researchers must wrestle as well as the theoretical and methodological issues at stake; many of the shortcomings of data collections stem from faulty execution of details rather than a lack of general understanding.

A book of this length obviously has to reflect a set of choices. Entire books can be, and have been, devoted to topics such as sampling, questionnaire design, and research on interviewers. Persons planning to carry out survey research projects will want to read further. Moreover, reading a book such as this, or any book, is no substitute for practical apprenticeship and training with experts who have both sound methodological backgrounds and extensive experience in the design and execution of surveys. However, there is an important role that this book, by itself, can play: namely, to provide a comprehensive overview of the sources of error and the range of methodological issues in survey data collection.

There are many people for whom such understanding will be appropriate and valuable. Certainly social scientists who use data collected by others in their work should have a sophisticated understanding of the sources of error. In the same way, people who read about statistics based on surveys need to understand the data collection process. This book identifies the questions that people who use data need to ask and have answered. In addition, it provides the overview that those who are considering purchasing or commissioning a survey need to have. In short, this book is intended to provide perspective and understanding to those who would be designers or users of survey research, at the same time providing a sound first step for those who actually may go about collecting data.

2

Sampling

How well a sample represents a population depends on the sample frame, the sample size, and the specific design of selection procedures. If probability sampling procedures are used, the precision of sample estimates can be calculated. This chapter describes various sampling procedures and their effects on the representativeness and precision of sample estimates. Two of the most common ways of sampling populations, area probability and random-digit dialing samples, are described in some detail.

There are occasions when the goal of information gathering is *not* to generate statistics about a population. Journalists, people developing products, political leaders, and others sometimes just want a general sense of people's feelings without great concern about numerical precision. Researchers do pilot studies to measure the range of ideas or opinions that people have or the way that variables seem to hang together. For these purposes, people who are readily available (friends, co-workers) or people who volunteer (magazine survey respondents, people who call talk shows) may be useful. Every effort to gather information does not require a strict probability sample survey. For the majority of occasions when surveys are undertaken, however, the goal is to develop statistics about a population. This chapter is about sampling when the goal is to produce numbers that can be subjected appropriately to the variety of statistical techniques available to social scientists. Although many of the same general principles apply to any sampling problem, the chapter focuses on sampling people.

The way to evaluate a sample is not by the results—the characteristics of the sample—but by examining the process by which it was selected. There are three key aspects of sample selection:

(1) The sample frame is the set of people that has a chance to be selected, given the sampling approach that is chosen. Statistically speaking, a sample only can be representative of the population included in the sample frame. One design issue is how well the sample frame corresponds to the population a researcher wants to describe.

(2) Probability sampling procedures must be used to designate individual units for inclusion in a sample. Each person should have a known chance of selection set by the sampling procedure. If researcher discretion or respondent characteristics such as respondent availability or initiative affect the chances of selection, there is no statistical basis for evaluating how well or how poorly the sample represents the population; commonly used approaches to calculating confidence intervals around sample estimates are not applicable.

(3) The details of the sample design, its size and the specific procedures used for selecting units, will influence directly the precision of sample estimates, that is, how closely a sample is likely to approximate the characteristics of the whole population.

These details of the sampling process, along with the rate at which information actually is obtained from those selected, constitute the facts needed to evaluate a survey sample.

Response rates are discussed in Chapter 3, which also includes a brief discussion of quota sampling, a common modification of probability sampling. In this chapter, we discuss sampling frames and probability sampling procedures. Several of the most common practical strategies for sampling people are described. Interested readers will find much more information on sampling in Kish (1965), Sudman (1976), and Kalton (1983). Researchers planning to carry out a survey almost always would be well advised to obtain the help of a sampling statistician. However, this chapter is intended to familiarize readers with the issues to which they should attend, and will likely encounter, when evaluating the sampling done for a survey.

THE SAMPLE FRAME

Any sample selection procedure will give some individuals a chance to be included in the sample while excluding others. The first step in evaluating the quality of a sample is to define the sample frame.

Although there is an infinite variety of ways to design sampling procedures, most sampling schemes fall into three general classes:

(1) Sampling is done from a more or less complete list of individuals in the population to be studied.

(2) Sampling is done from a set of people who go somewhere or do something that enables them to be sampled. For example, one might sample patients who received medical care from a physician or people who attended a meeting. In those cases, there is not an advance list from which sampling occurs; rather the creation of the list and the process of sampling occur simultaneously.

(3) Sampling is done in two or more stages, with the first stage involving sampling something other than the individuals finally to be selected. In one or more steps, these primary units are sampled, and eventually a list of individuals (or other sampling units) is created, from which a final sample selection is made. One of the most common such sampling schemes is to select housing units, with no prior information about who lives there, as a first stage of selecting a sample of people living in those housing units. These multistage procedures will be described in more detail later in this chapter.

There are three characteristics of a sample frame that a researcher should evaluate:

(1) Comprehensiveness. A sample can only be representative of the sample frame—that is, the population that actually had a chance to be selected. Most sampling approaches leave out at least a few people from the population the researcher wants to study. For example, household-based samples exclude people who live in group quarters such as dormitories, prisons, and nursing homes as well as those who are homeless. Available general lists, such as people with driver's licenses, registered voters, and homeowners, are even more exclusive. Although they cover large segments of some populations, they also omit major segments with distinctive characteristics. As a specific example, published telephone directories omit those without telephones, those who have requested that their numbers not be published, and those who have been assigned a telephone number since the most recent directory was published. In some central cities, such exclusions amount to almost 50 percent of all households. In such cities, a sample drawn from a telephone directory would be representative of only about half the population.

A key part of evaluating any sampling scheme is determining the percentage of the study population that has a chance of being selected, and the extent to which those excluded are distinctive. Very often a researcher may make a choice between an easier or less expensive way of sampling a population that leaves out some people, or a more expensive strategy that is also more comprehensive. If a researcher is considering sampling from a list, it is particularly important to evaluate the list to find out in detail how it was compiled and how updating was carried out.

(2) Giving each person in the sample frame a known probability of selection is a second way in which a sampling scheme should be evaluated. A procedure that samples records of visits to a doctor over

a year may give individuals who visit the doctor numerous times a higher chance of selection unless some adjustment is made. It is not necessary that a sampling scheme give every member of the sampling frame the same chance of selection, as would be the case if each individual appeared once and only once on a list. It is essential, however, that the researcher be able to find out the probability of selection for each individual selected. This may be done at the time of sample selection by examination of the list. It also may be possible to find out the probability of selection at the time of data collection. In the above example of sampling patients by sampling doctor visits, if the researcher asks selected patients the number of visits to the physician they had in a year, it would be possible to adjust the data at the time of analysis to take into account the different chances of selection. However, if it is not possible to know the probability of selection of each selected individual, it is not possible to estimate accurately the relationship between the sample statistics and the population from which it was drawn.

(3) The efficiency of a sampling scheme is the last criterion. In some cases, sampling frames include units that are not among those that the researcher wants to sample. Assuming that eligible persons can be identified at the point of data collection, being too comprehensive is not a problem. Hence a perfectly appropriate way to sample elderly people living in households is to draw a sample of all households, find out if there are elderly persons living in selected households, then exclude those households with no elderly residents. The only question about such designs is whether or not they are cost effective.

Because the ability to generalize from a sample is limited by the sample frame, when reporting results the researcher must tell readers who was and was not given a chance to be selected, how those omitted were distinctive, and whether or not there were any sampled people for whom the chances of selection were not known.

SELECTING A ONE-STAGE SAMPLE

Once a researcher has made a decision about a sample frame or approach to getting a sample, the next question is specifically how to select the individual units to be included. In the next few sections we discuss the various ways that samplers typically draw samples.

Simple Random Sampling

Simple random sampling is in some sense the prototype of population sampling. The simplest ways of calculating statistics about samples assume that a simple random sample was drawn. Simple random sampling approximates drawing a sample out of a hat: Members of a population are selected, one at a time, independently of one another, without replacement; once a unit is selected, it has no further chance to be selected.

Operationally, drawing a simple random sample requires a numbered list of the population. For simplicity, assume that each person in the population appears once and only once.

If there were 8,500 people on the list, and the goal was to select a simple random sample of 100, the procedure would be straightforward. People on the list would be numbered from 1 to 8,500. Then a computer, a table of random numbers, or some other generator of random numbers would be used to produce 100 different numbers in the range from 0001 to 8,500. The individuals corresponding to the 100 numbers chosen would constitute a simple random sample of that population of 8,500.

Systematic Samples

Although simple random samples are easy to understand, in practice they are relatively rare. Unless a list is short, has all units prenumbered, or is computerized so that it can be numbered easily, drawing a simple random sample as described above can be laborious. With most lists, there is a way to use a variation called systematic sampling that will have precision equivalent to a simple random sample and will be mechanically easier to draw. Moreover, the benefits of stratification discussed in the next section can be accomplished more easily through systematic sampling.

When drawing a systematic sample from a list, the researcher first determines the number of entries on the list and the number of elements from the list that are to be selected. Dividing the latter by the former will produce a fraction.

Thus if there are 8,500 people on a list and a sample of 100 is required, 1/85 of the list is to be included in the sample; one out of every 85 persons on the list is to be selected.

In order to select a systematic sample, a start point is designated by choosing a random number from 1 to 85. The randomized start ensures that it is a chance selection process. Given that start, the researcher proceeds to take every 85th person on the list.

Most statistics books warn that a recurring pattern or periodicity in a list that corresponds to the sampling interval can produce a biased sample. Such patterns are rare, and it is unusual not to be able to use a systematic approach to sampling from a list. An example of the kind of pattern to look out for is that corner houses on blocks tend to be more expensive. Hence researchers need to avoid choosing a selection procedure that consistently would select corner houses, but such patterns are not hard to avoid. The characteristics of a list should be studied carefully before deciding on a systematic sampling procedure or any other sampling procedure.

Stratified Samples

When a simple random sample is drawn, each new selection is independent, unaffected by any selections that came before. As a result of this process, any of the characteristics of the sample may, by chance, differ somewhat from the population from which it is drawn.

Generally, little is known about the characteristics of individual population members before data collection. However, it is not uncommon for at least a few characteristics of a population to be identifiable at the time of sampling. When that is the case, there is the possibility of structuring the sampling process to reduce the normal sampling variation, thereby producing a sample that is more likely to reflect the total population than a simple random sample. The process by which this is done is called stratification.

Example. Suppose one had a list of college students. The list is arranged alphabetically. Members of different classes are mixed throughout the list.

If the list identifies the particular class to which a student belongs, it would be possible to rearrange the list, putting freshmen first, then sophomores, then juniors, and finally seniors together. If the sampling design calls for selecting a sample of 1 in 10 of the members on the list, the rearrangement would ensure that exactly 1/10 of the freshmen were selected, 1/10 of the sophomores, and so forth. On the other hand, if a simple random sample were selected from the list, or a systematic sample from the alphabetical list, the proportion of the sample in the freshman year would be subject to normal sampling variability and could be slightly higher or lower than was the case for the population. Stratifying in advance ensures that the sample will have exactly the same proportions in each class as the whole population.

Consider the task of estimating the average age of the student body. The class in which a student is a member almost certainly is correlated with age. Although there still will be some variability in sample estimates because of the sampling procedure, structuring the representation of classes in the sample also will constrain considerably the extent to which the age of the sample will differ by chance from the population as a whole.

Almost all samples of populations of geographic areas are stratified by some regional variable so they will be distributed in the same way as the population as a whole. National samples typically are stratified by region of the country and also by urban, suburban, and rural locations. Lists of employees typically are stratified by occupational classification of some sort.

Stratification only increases the precision of estimates of variables to which the stratification variables are related. Since some degree of stratification is relatively simple to accomplish, however, and since it never hurts the precision of a sample, it usually is a desirable feature of a sample design.

Differential Probabilities of Selection

Using a simple random sample or systematic sampling procedure, a group that constitutes 10 percent of a population will constitute about 10 percent of a selected sample. With such a sample design, if a researcher wanted a sample of at least 100 of a population subgroup that constituted 10 percent of the population, a simple random sampling approach would require an overall sample of 1,000. Moreover, if a researcher decided to increase the sample size of that subgroup to 150, it would entail taking an additional 500 interviews into the sample, bringing the total to 1,500.

Obviously, there are occasions when increasing a sample in this way is not very cost effective. In the latter example, if a researcher is satisfied with the size of the samples of other groups, the design adds 450 unwanted interviews in order to add 50 interviews that are wanted. In some cases, therefore, an appropriate design is to select some subgroup at a higher rate than the rest of the population.

Example. Suppose that only 10 percent of the students at a particular college were black. Thus a sample of 500 students would include 50 black students. To make meaningful comparisons between black and white students, there was a desire for a minimum of 100 black respondents.

If black students could be identified in advance, one could select black students at twice the rate at which other students were selected. In this way, rather than adding 500 interviews to increase the sample by 50 blacks, an additional 50 interviews, over the basic sample of 500, would produce a total of about 100 interviews with blacks.

Thus when making black-white comparisons, one would have the precision provided by samples of 100 black respondents and 450 white respondents. To combine these samples, the researcher would have to give black respondents a weight of 1/2 that given to others to compensate for the fact that they were sampled at twice the rate of the rest of the population.[1]

Example	Whites	Blacks
Number in population	4500	500
Percentage of population	90	10
Sampling fraction	1/10	1/5
No selected in sample	450	100
Unweighted percentage of sample	81.8	18.2
WT (to adjust for probability of selection)	1	1/2
Weighted number in sample	450	50
Weighted percentage of sample	90	10

Even if individual members of a subgroup of interest cannot be identified with certainty in advance of sampling, sometimes the basic approach outlined above can be applied. For instance, it is most unusual to have a general household list that identifies race in advance of contact. It is not uncommon, however, for black families to be more concentrated in some neighborhood areas than others. In that instance, a researcher may be able to sample households in areas that are predominantly black at a higher than average rate to increase the number of black respondents. Again, when any group is given a chance of selection different from other members of the population, appropriate compensatory weighting is required in order to generate accurate population statistics for the combined or total sample.

MULTISTAGE SAMPLING

Overview

When there is no adequate list of the individuals in a population and no way to get at the population directly, multistage sampling provides a useful approach.

In the absence of a direct sampling source, a strategy is needed for linking population members to some kind of grouping that can be sampled. These groupings can be sampled at a first stage. Lists then are made of individual members of selected groups, with possibly a further selection from the created list at the second (or later) stage of sampling. The following section illustrates the general strategy for multistage sampling by describing its use in three of the most common types of situations in which a list is not available.

Three Common Applications

Sampling students from schools. If one wanted to draw a sample of all students enrolled in the public schools of a particular city, it would not be surprising to find that there was not a complete list of such individuals. There is, however, a sample frame that enables one to "get at" and include all the students in the population: namely, the list of all the public schools in that city. Since every individual in the study population can be attached to one and only one of those units, a perfectly acceptable sample of students can be selected using a two-stage strategy, first selecting schools, and then selecting students from within those schools.

Given the following data:

    20,000 students
    40 schools
    Desired sample = 2,000 = 1/10 of students

Four different designs or approaches to sampling are presented below. Each would yield a probability sample of 2,000 students.

	Probability of Selection at Stage 1	×	Probability of Selection at Stage 2	=	Overall Probability of Selection
(a) Select all schools, list all students, select 1/10 students in each school.	1/1	×	1/10	=	1/10
(b) Select 1/2 the schools, then select 1/5 of all students in them.	1/2	×	1/5	=	1/10
(c) Select 1/5 schools, then 1/2 of all students in them.	1/5	×	1/2	=	1/10
(d) Select 1/10 schools, then collect information about all students in them	1/10	×	1/1	=	1/10

The four approaches listed all yield samples of 2,000; all give each student an equal chance (1 in 10) of selection. The difference is that from top to bottom the designs are increasingly less expensive—with each approach, lists have to be collected from fewer schools and fewer schools need to be visited. At the same time, the precision of each sample is likely to decline as fewer schools are sampled and more students are sampled per school. The effect of this and other multistage designs on the precision of sample estimates is discussed in more detail in a later section of this chapter.

Area probability sampling. Area probability sampling is one of the most generally useful multistage strategies because of its wide applicability. It can be used to sample any population that can be defined geographicaly; for example, the people living in a neighborhood, a city, or a country. The basic approach is to divide the total target land area into exhaustive, mutually exclusive subareas with identifiable boundaries. A sample of subareas is drawn. A list then is made of housing units in selected subareas, and a sample of listed units is drawn. As a final stage, all people in selected housing units may be included in the sample, or they may be listed and sampled as well.

This approach will work for jungles, deserts, sparsely populated rural areas, or downtown areas in central cities. The specific steps to drawing such a sample properly can be very complicated. However, the basic principles can be illustrated by describing how one could sample the population of a city using city blocks as the primary subarea units to be selected at the first stage of sampling.

Suppose we are given the following data:

A city consists of 400 blocks.

There are 20,000 housing units located on those blocks.

Desired sample—2,000 housing units—1/10 of all housing units.

Given this information, a sample of households could be selected using a strategy parallel to the above selection of students. In the first stage of sampling, blocks are selected. Second, housing units on selected blocks are listed and selected from the lists. Two approaches to selecting housing units are:

	Probability of Selection at Stage 1	×	Probability of Selection at Stage 2	=	Overall Probability of Selection
(a) Select 80 blocks (1/5), then take 1/2 of units on those blocks.	1/5	×	1/2	=	1/10

(b) Select 40 blocks (1/10),
      then take all units on   1/10   ×   1/1   =   1/10
      those blocks.

   Parallel to the school example, example a, involving more blocks, is more expensive than b; it also is likely to produce more precise sample estimates for a sample of a given size.

   None of the above sample schemes takes into account the size of the Stage 1 unit or groupings (i.e., the size of the blocks or schools). Big schools and big blocks are selected at the same rate as small ones. If a fixed fraction of each selected group is to be taken at the last stage, there will be more interviews taken from selected big schools or big blocks than from small ones; the size of the samples taken at the last stages (cluster sizes) will be very divergent.

   If there is information available about the size of the Stage 1 units, it is usually good to use it. Sample designs of a given size usually provide the most precise estimates if the number of units taken in each cluster at the last stage of selection is approximately equal. To do this, one should sample the Stage 1 units *proportionate to their size*.

   The following example shows the way blocks could be sampled proportionate to size as the first stage of an area probability approach to sampling housing units. The same approach could be applied to the school example above, treating schools in a way analogous to blocks in the following process.

   (1) Decide how many units are to be selected at the *last* stage of sampling—the average cluster size. Let us choose 10, for example.

   (2) Make an estimate of the number of housing units in each Stage 1 unit (block).

   (3) Order the blocks so that geographically adjacent or otherwise similar blocks are contiguous. This effectively stratifies the sampling to improve the samples, as discussed above.

   (4) Create a cumulative count across all blocks of estimated housing units. A table like the one below will result.

Block Number	Estimated Housing Units	Cumulative Housing Units	"Hits" (Random Start = 70; Interval = 100 HUs)
1	43	43	—
2	87	130	70
3	109	239	170
4	27	266	—
5	15	281	270

(5) Determine the interval between clusters. If we want to select 1 in 10 housing units and a cluster of about 10 on each selected block, we need an interval of 100 housing units between clusters. Put another way, instead of taking one unit at an interval of every tenth house, we take 10 units at an interval of every 100 houses; the rate is the same, but the pattern is "clustered."

(6) With a random start (from 1 to 100, the interval), proceed systematically through the cumulative count, designating the primary units (or blocks) "hit" in this first stage of selection. In the example, the random start missed block 1; the 70th housing unit was in block 2; the 170th housing unit was in block 3; the 270th housing unit skipped block 4 and was located in block 5.

A list then is made of the housing units on the selected blocks 2, 3, and 5—usually by sending a person to visit the blocks. The next step is to select housing units from those lists. If we were sure the estimates of the sizes of blocks were accurate, we simply could select 10 units off each selected block, either using simple random or systematic sampling.[2]

Block Number	Estimated Housing Units	Probability of Selecting Block (Stage 1)	×	Probability of Selecting House Once Block Selected (Stage 2)	=	Overall Probability
2	87	87/100	×	10/87	=	1/10
3	109	109/100	×	10/109	=	1/10
5	15	15/100	×	10/15	=	1/10

Note in the example that there were 87 chances in 100 (the interval of selection) that block 2 would be "hit" at Stage 1 of selection. Once it was "hit," the odds of taking a specific house on that block were 10/87. The product of those two fractions is 1/10 for block 2 and for every other block. Notice that the odds of selecting a housing unit are unaffected by the size of the block it is on.

It is common for estimates of the size of Stage 1 units such as blocks to be somewhat in error. We can correct for such errors by calculating the rate at which houses are to be selected from blocks as:

$$\text{rate of h.u. selection on block} = \frac{\text{ave. cluster size}}{\text{estimated \# h.u.'s on block}} = \text{(on block 2)} \ \frac{10}{87} = \frac{1}{8.7}$$

In our example, we would take 1 per 8.7 houses on block 2, 1 per 10.9 houses on block 3, and 1 per 1.5 houses on block 5. If a block is bigger than expected (e.g., due to new construction), more than 10 houses will be drawn; if it is smaller than expected (e.g., due to demolition), fewer than 10 units will be drawn. If it is exactly what we expected (87 on block 2), we take 10 homes (87 ÷ 8.7 = 10). In this way, the procedure is self-correcting for errors in initial estimates of block size, while maintaining the same chance of selection for units on all blocks.

The area probability sample approach can be used to sample any geographically defined population. Although the steps are more complicated as the area gets bigger, the approach is the same. The key steps to remember are the following:

(1) All areas must be given some chance of selection. Combine areas where no units are expected with adjacent areas to ensure a chance of selection; new construction may have occurred or estimates may be wrong.

(2) The probability of selecting a block (or other land area) times the probability of selecting a housing unit from a selected block should be constant across all blocks.

Finally, even careful field listers will miss some housing units. Therefore, it is good practice to include checks for missed units at the time of data collection.

Random-Digit Dialing

Random-digit dialing provides an alternative way to draw a sample of housing units in order to sample the people in those households.

Suppose the 20,000 housing units in the above example are covered by six telephone exchanges. One could draw a probability sample of 10 percent of the housing units that have a telephone as follows:

(1) There is a total of 60,000 telephone numbers in those 6 exchanges (10,000 per exchange). Select 6,000 of those numbers (10 percent), drawing 1,000 randomly generated, four-digit numbers per exchange.

(2) Dial all 6,000 numbers. Not all the numbers will be household numbers; in fact, many of the numbers will not be working, will be disconnected or temporarily not in service, or will be businesses. Since 10 percent of all possible telephone numbers that could serve the area have been called, about 10 percent of all the households with telephones in that area will be reached by calling the sample of numbers.

This is the basic random-digit dialing approach to sampling. The obvious disadvantage of this approach is the large number of unfruitful calls. Nationally, less than 25 percent of possible numbers are associated with residential housing units. The rate is about 30 percent in urban areas and about 10 percent in rural areas. Waksberg (1978) has developed a method of taking advantage of the fact that telephone numbers are assigned in groups. Each group is defined by a three-digit area code, an exchange, and two additional numbers. By carrying out an initial screening of numbers, then calling additional random numbers only within the groups of 100 numbers (area code-555-12--) where a residential number was found, the rate of hitting housing units can be raised to over 60 percent.

Listings in a telephone directory also may be used as a surrogate for the initial screening. Use of a directory, however, is subject to the assumption that listed numbers are distributed in the same way as all currently working residential numbers. Newly developed areas may be assigned new groups of numbers that may be underrepresented among listed numbers.

There are two problems to note about the random-digit dialing approach to sampling. First, it omits those who live in housing units without telephones. Nationally, that is about 5 percent of the households. In some areas—particularly central cities or rural areas—the rate of omission may be greater than that.

Second, it is a problematic way to sample people within small areas where telephone exchanges do not correspond to area boundaries. Unless the telephone exchanges exactly correspond to the study area, interviewers will need to have respondents tell them whether or not they live in the study area. Respondents who live in small, poorly defined areas—such as neighborhoods—may perform that task unreliably.

Like any particular sampling approach, random-digit dialing is not the solution to all problems. In some urban areas, leaving out people without phones would be a serious compromise, whereas in other areas it is almost no compromise at all. The significance of leaving out that distinctive group without telephones also will vary with the topic of the study. The pros and cons of telephone interviewing will be discussed in Chapter 4. However, the introduction of random-digit dialing is one tool in the survey researcher's arsenal that has made a major contribution to expanding survey research capabilities.

Respondent Selection

Both area probability samples and random-digit dialing designate a sample of housing units. There is then the further question of whom in the household should be interviewed.

The best decision depends on what is being studied and what kind of information is being gathered. In some studies, the information is being gathered about the household and about all the people in the household. If the information is easy to report, perhaps any adult who is home can answer the questions. If the information is more specialized, the researcher may want to interview the household member who is most knowledgeable. For example, in the National Health Interview Survey the "person who knows the most about the health of the family" is to be the respondent.

There are, however, many things that an individual can report only for himself or herself. In particular, researchers almost universally feel that no individual can report feelings, opinions, or knowledge for some other person.

When a study includes variables for which only self-reporting is appropriate, the sampling process must go beyond selecting households to sampling specific individuals within those households.

One approach is to interview every eligible person in a household. Because of homogeneity within households, however, and also concerns about one respondent influencing a later respondent's answers, it is more common to designate a single respondent per household.

Obviously, taking the person who happens to answer the phone or the door would be a nonprobabilistic and probably biased way of selecting individuals; interviewer discretion, respondent discretion, and availability (which is related to working status, life-style, age) would all affect who turned out to be the respondent. The key principle of probability sampling is that selection is carried out through some chance or random procedure that designates specific people.

The procedure for generating a probabilistic selection of respondents within households involves three steps:

(1) Ascertain how many people living in a household are eligible to be respondents (e.g., How many are 18 or older?).
(2) Number these in a consistent way in all households (e.g., order by increasing age).
(3) Have a procedure that objectively designates one person to be respondent.

Kish (1949) created a detailed procedure for designating respondents using a set of randomized tables that still is used widely today. The critical features of such a system are that no discretion be involved and that all eligible people in selected households have a known (nonzero) probability of selection.

It should be noted that when only one person is interviewed in a household, a differential rate of selection is introduced. If an adult lives in a one-adult household, he or she will be the respondent with certainty if the household is selected. In contrast, an adult living in a three-adult household only will be the respondent one-third of the time.

As with any design that involves sampling one identifiable group at a rate different from others, the solution to producing unbiased population estimates is to weight by the reciprocal of the probability of selection. In this case, one simply weights adults from three-adult households by three, adults from two-adult households by two, and so forth. This is used in addition to any other weights the sample design may require.

Empirically, this weighting often does not affect sample estimates. Many variables are unassociated with the number of adults in a household. However, there are variables that are associated strongly with the number of adults in a household. An outstanding example is marital status; married people are much more likely to live in two-adult households than single people. The careful researcher will check the variables to be studied to see if they are affected by weighting. If not, weighting may be dispensed with. However, with the use of computers, weighting is not difficult and is always appropriate.

MAKING ESTIMATES FROM SAMPLES
AND SAMPLING ERRORS

The sampling strategies presented above were chosen because they are among the most commonly used and they illustrate the major sampling design options. A probability sampling scheme eventually will designate a specific set of households or individuals without researcher or respondent discretion. The basic tools available to the researcher are simple random and systematic sampling, which are modified by stratification, unequal rates of selection, and clustering. The choice of a sampling strategy rests in part on feasibility and costs. It also involves the precision of sample estimates.

A major reason for using probability sampling methods is to permit use of a variety of statistical tools to estimate the precision of sample estimates. In this section, we discuss the calculation of such estimates and how they are affected by features of the sample design.

Researchers usually have no interest in the characteristics of a sample per se. The reason for collecting data about a sample is to reach conclusions about an entire population. The statistical and design issues in this chapter are considered in the context of how much confidence one can have that the characteristics of a sample accurately describe the population as a whole.

Many common images have been used to explain probability theory. Perhaps the easiest one to understand is flipping a coin. If a perfectly fair coin is flipped ten times, on any given set of ten flips it may not come out exactly five heads and five tails. Sometimes there will be six heads, occasionally seven heads and once in a very great while one even might get ten heads. In essence, one could think of any ten flips as one of many possible samples. If one executed a series of ten flips, flipping the coin ten times and calculating the number of heads, flipping it another ten times and keeping track of the number of heads again, and so forth, a distribution would result. If it was a fair coin, there would be more samples of ten flips that produced five heads than any other number. There also would be a distribution around five heads with the extremes, ten heads and no heads, occurring at the lowest frequency.

Although some sources of error in surveys are biasing and produce systematically distorted figures, sampling error is a random (and hence not a systematically biasing) result of sampling. When probability procedures are used to select a sample, it is possible to calculate how much sample estimates will vary by chance due to sampling. If an infinite number of samples are drawn, the sample estimates of descriptive statistics such as means will form a normal distribution around the true population value. The larger the size of the sample and the less the variance of what is being measured, the more tightly the sample estimates will bunch around the true population value; the more accurate will be a sample-based estimate. This variation around the true value, stemming from the fact that by chance samples may differ from the population as a whole, is called sampling error. Estimating the limits of the confidence one can have in a sample estimate, given normal chance sampling variability, is one important part of evaluating figures derived from surveys.

The design of sample selection, specifically whether it involves stratification, clustering, or unequal probabilities of selection, affects the estimates of sampling error for a sample of a given size. However, the usual approach to describing sampling errors is to calculate what they would be for a simple random sample, then to calculate the effects of deviations from a simple random sampling design. Hence we begin by describing the calculation of sampling errors for simple random samples.

CALCULATING SAMPLING ERRORS
FOR SIMPLE RANDOM SAMPLES

This is not a textbook on sampling statistics. However, estimating the amount of error one can expect from a particular sample design is a basic part of the survey design process. Moreover, researchers routinely provide readers with guidelines regarding error due to sampling, guidelines both the knowledgeable reader and user of survey research data should know and understand. To this end, a sense of how sampling error is calculated is a necessary part of understanding the total survey process.

Although the same logic applies to all statistics calculated from a sample, the most common sample survey estimates are means or averages. The statistic most often used to describe sampling error is called the *standard error* (of a mean). It is the standard deviation of the distribution of sample estimates of means that would be formed if an infinite number of samples of a given size were drawn. When the value of a standard error has been estimated, one can say that 67 percent of the means of samples of a given size and design will fall within the range of ± 1 standard error of the true population mean; 95 percent of such samples will fall within the range of ± 2 standard errors. The latter figure (± 2 standard errors) often is reported as the "confidence interval" around a sample estimate.

The estimation of the standard error of a mean is calculated from the variance of a measure and the size of the sample from which it was estimated.

$$SE = \sqrt{\frac{Var}{n}}$$

SE   = standard error of a mean

Var   = the variance, the sum of the squared deviations from the sample mean

n   = size of the sample

The most common kind of mean calculated from a sample survey is probably a proportion, that is, the percentage of a sample that has a certain characteristic or gives a certain response. It may be useful to show how a proportion is the mean of a two-value distribution.

Mean: A mean is an average. It is calculated as the sum of the values divided by the number of cases: $\Sigma X/n$.

Now suppose there are only two values, 0 and 1. There are 50 cases in a sample; 20 say "yes" they are married, the rest say "no" they are not married. If there are 20 "yeses" and 30 "nos," calculate the mean as

$$\Sigma X = 20 \times 1 + 30 \times 0 = 20; \frac{\Sigma X}{n} = \frac{20}{50} = .40$$

A proportion statement, such as 40 percent are married, is just a statement about the mean of a 1/0 distribution. The mean is .40.

The calculation of standard errors of proportions is facilitated by the fact that the *variance of a proportion* can be calculated readily as p $\times (1 - p)$, where p = proportion having a characteristic (say, the 40 percent married in the above example) and $(1 - p)$ is the proportion who lack the characteristic (the 60 percent not married).

We have already seen that the standard error of an estimate is as follows:

$$\sqrt{\frac{Var}{n}}$$

Since p $(1 - p)$ is the variance of a proportion,

$$\sqrt{\frac{p(1 - p)}{n}}$$

is the standard error of a proportion. In our previous example, with 40 percent of a sample of 50 being married, the standard error of that estimate would be as follows:

$$\sqrt{\frac{p(1-p)}{n}} = \sqrt{\frac{.40 \times .60}{50}} = \sqrt{\frac{.24}{50}} = .07$$

Thus we would estimate that the odds are .67 (i.e., ± 1 standard error from the sample mean) that the true population figure (the proportion of the whole population that is married) is between .33 and .47 (.40 $\pm$ .07). We are 95 percent confident that the true population figure lies within two standard errors of our sample mean, between .26 and .54 (.40 $\pm$ .14).

Table 2.1 is a generalized table of sampling errors for samples of various sizes and for various proportions, provided that samples were selected as simple random samples. Each number in the table represents two standard errors of a proportion. Given knowledge (or an estimate) of the proportion of a sample that gives a particular answer, the table gives 95 percent confidence interval for various sample sizes. In the example above, with 50 cases yielding a sample estimate of 40 percent married, the table reports a confidence interval near 14, as we calculated. If a sample of about 100 cases produced an estimate that 20 percent were married, the table says we can be 95 percent sure that the true figure is 20 percent ±8 percentage points (12 to 28 percent). Several points about the table are worth noting.

First, it can be seen that increasingly large samples always reduce sampling errors.

Second, it also can be seen that adding a given number of cases to a sample reduces sampling error a great deal more when the sample is small than when it is comparatively large. For example, adding 50 cases to a sample of 50 produces a quite noticeable reduction in sampling error. However, adding 50 cases to a sample of 500 produces a virtually unnoticeable improvement in the overall precision of sample estimates.

Third, it can be seen that the absolute size of the sampling error is greatest around proportions of .5 and decreases when the proportion of a sample having a characteristic approaches 0 (or 100) percent. We have seen that standard errors are related directly to variances. The variance—$p \times (1 - p)$—is smaller as the proportions get further from .5.

Fourth, Table 2.1 and the equations on which it is based apply to samples using simple random sampling procedures. Most samples of general populations are not simple random samples. The extent to which the particular sample design will affect calculations of sampling error varies from design to design and for different variables in the same survey. More often than not, Table 2.1 will constitute an underestimate of the sampling error for a general population sample.

Finally, it should be emphasized that the variability reflected in Table 2.1 describes potential for error that comes from the fact of sampling rather than collecting information about every individual in a population. Those calculations do not include estimates of error from any other aspects of the survey process.

EFFECTS OF OTHER SAMPLE DESIGN FEATURES
ON SAMPLING ERRORS

The preceding discussion describes the calculation of sampling errors for simple random samples. Estimates of sampling errors will be affected by different sampling procedures.

Systematic sampling should produce sampling errors equivalent to simple random samples if there is no stratification.

Stratified samples will produce sampling errors that are *lower* than those associated with simple random samples of the same size for variables that are more homogeneous within strata than in the population as a whole.

Unequal rates of selection (selecting subgroups in the population at different rates) are designed to increase the precision of estimates for oversampled subgroups, but will produce sampling errors for the whole sample that are *higher* than those associated with simple random samples of the same size for variables that are more homogeneous within oversampled groups than in the population as a whole.

Clustering will produce sampling errors that are *higher* than those associated with simple random samples of the same size for variables that are more homogeneous within clusters than in the population as a whole. Also the larger the size of the cluster at the last stage, the larger the impact on sampling errors.

One clear complexity of sampling is anticipating the effects of design features on the precision of estimates. They differ from study to study and for different variables in the same survey.

To illustrate, suppose every house on selected blocks was the same with respect to type of construction and whether or not it was owner occupied. Once we had interviewed at the first selected housing unit on a block and learned that it was a single-family house and was owner occupied, the additional interviews on that block would yield absolutely no new information about the rate of home ownership or the rate of single-family houses in the population as a whole. For that reason, whether we took one interview per block or twenty interviews per block, the reliability of our estimates of those variables would be exactly the same, basically proportionate to the number of blocks from which we took any interviews at all. At the other extreme, the height of adults is likely to be unrelated to what block a person lives on. If clusters of interviews on a block are as hetergeneous as the population as a whole, clustering would not decrease the precision of estimates of height from a sample of a given size. One has to look at the nature of the clusters or strata and what estimates are to be made in order to evaluate the likely effect of clustering on sampling errors.

The effects of the sample design on sampling errors often are unappreciated. It is not uncommon to see reports of confidence intervals that assume simple random sampling when the design was clustered.

It also is not a simple matter to anticipate design effects beforehand or to calculate them after a study is complete. As noted, the effects of the sample design on sampling errors are different for every variable; their calculation particularly is complicated when a sample design has several deviations from simple random sampling such as clustering and stratification. Since the ability to calculate sampling errors is one of the principal strengths of the survey method, it is important that a statistician be involved in a survey with a complex sample design to ensure that sampling errors are calculated and reported appropriately.

Finally, the appropriateness of any sample design feature can be evaluated only in the context of the overall survey objectives. Clustered designs are likely to save money both in sampling (listing) and in data collection. Moreover, it is common to find many variables for which clustering does not inflate the sampling errors much. Oversampling one or more groups often is a cost-effective design. As with most issues discussed in this book, the important point is for a researcher to be aware of the potential costs and benefits of the options and to weigh them in the context of all the design options and the main purposes of the survey.

HOW BIG SHOULD A SAMPLE BE?

Of the many issues involved in sample design, one of the most common questions posed to a survey methodologist is how big a survey sample should be. Before providing an approach to answering that question, perhaps it is appropriate to discuss three common but inappropriate ways of answering that question.

One common misconception is that the adequacy of a sample depends heavily on the fraction of the population included in that sample; that somehow 1 percent or 5 percent or some percentage of a population will make a sample credible.

The estimates of sampling errors discussed above do not take into account the fraction of a population included in a sample. The sampling error estimates from the preceding equations and from Table 2.1 and can be reduced by the value $(1 - f)$, where f = the fraction of the population included in a sample.

When one is sampling 10 percent or more of a population, this adjustment can have a discernable effect on sampling error estimates. The vast majority of survey samples, however, involve very small fractions of populations. In such instances, small increments in the fraction of the population included in a sample will have no effect on the ability of a researcher to generalize from a sample to a population.

The converse of that principle also should be noted. The size of the population from which a sample of a particular size is drawn has virtually no impact on how well that sample is likely to describe the population. A sample of 150 people will describe a population of 15,000 or 15 million with virtually the same degree of accuracy, assuming all other aspects of the sample design and sampling procedures were the same.

Compared to the total sample size and other design features such as clustering, the impact of the fraction of a population sampled on sampling errors is typically trivial. It is most unusual for it to be an important consideration when deciding on a sample size.

A second approach to deciding on sample size is somewhat easier to understand. Some people have been exposed to so-called "standard" survey studies and from these have derived a "typical" or "appropriate" sample size. Thus some people will say that good national survey samples generally are 1,500 or that community samples are 500. Of course, it is not foolish to look at what other competent researchers have considered to be adequate sample sizes of a particular population. However, the sample size decision, like most other design decisions, must be made on a case-by-case basis, considering the variety of goals to be achieved by a particular study and taking into account numerous other aspects of the research design.

A third wrong approach to deciding on sample size is the most important one to address, for its origin is easy to find; it can be found in many statistical textbooks. The approach goes like this: A researcher should decide how much margin of error he or she can tolerate or how much precision is required of estimates. Once one knows the need for precision, one simply uses a table such as Table 2.1, or appropriate variations thereon, to calculate the sample size needed to achieve the desired level of precision.

In some theoretical sense, there is nothing wrong with this approach. In practice, however, it provides little help to most researchers trying to design real studies.

First, it is unusual to base a sample size decision on the need for precision of a single estimate. Most survey studies are designed to make a variety of estimates. The needed precision for these estimates is likely to vary from measure to measure.

In addition, it is unusual for a researcher to be able to specify a desired level of precision in more than the most general way. It is only the exception, rather than the common situation, when a specific acceptable margin for error can be specified in advance.

TABLE 2.1
Confidence Ranges for Variability Due to Sampling*

	Percentage of Sample with Characteristic				
Sample Size	5/95	10/90	20/80	30/70	50/50
35	7	10	14	15	17
50	6	8	11	13	14
75	5	7	9	11	12
100	4	6	8	9	10
200	3	4	6	6	7
300	3	3	5	5	6
500	2	3	4	4	4
1000	1	2	3	3	3
1500	1	2	2	2	2

NOTE: Chances are 95 in 100 that the real population figure lies in the range defined by ± number indicated in table, given percentage of sample reporting characteristic and number of sample cases on which the percentage is based.

*This table describes variability due to sampling. Errors due to nonresponse or reporting errors are not reflected in this table. In addition, this table assumes a simple random sample. Estimates may be subject to more variability than this table indicates due to the sample design or the influence of interviewers on the answers they obtained; stratification might reduce the sampling errors below those indicated here.

Even in the latter unusual case, the above approach implies that sampling error is the only or main source of error in a survey estimate. When a required level of precision from a sample survey is specified, it generally ignores the fact that there will be error from sources other than sampling. In such cases, the calculation of precision based on sampling error alone is an unrealistic oversimplification. Moreover, given fixed resources, increasing the sample size even may decrease precision by reducing resources devoted to response rates, questionnaire design, or the quality of data collection.

Estimates of samplng error, which are related to sample size, do play a role in analyses of how big a sample should be. However, the role is complicated.

The first prerequisite for determining a sample size is an analysis plan. The key component of that analysis plan usually is not an estimate of confidence intervals for the overall sample but rather an outline of the subgroups within the total population for which separate estimates are required, together with some etimates of the fraction of the population that will fall into those subgroups. Typically, the design process moves quickly to identifying the smaller groups within the population for which figures are needed. The researcher then estimates how large a sample will be required in order to provide a minimally adequate sample of these small subgroups. Most sample size decisions do not focus on estimates for the total population. Rather they are concentrated on the minimum sample sizes that can be tolerated for the smallest subgroups of importance.

To state that in concrete terms, a researcher is likely to ask whether or not estimates must be made separately for males and females. For a national sample, the researcher is likely to wonder whether or not separate regional estimates are required. Further, to what extent will one want to look at males and females or different educational groups within regions? What kind of breakdowns of education or income groups will be needed? What about ethnic groups? What fraction of the population is black?

The process then turns to Table 2.1, not at the high end but at the low end of the sample size continuum. Are 50 observations adequate? If one studies Table 2.1, one can see that precision increases rather steadily up to sample sizes of 150 to 200. After that point, there is a much more modest gain to increasing sample size.

Like most decisions relating to research design, there is seldom a definitive answer about how large a sample should be for any given study. There are many ways to increase the reliability of survey estimates. Increasing sample size is one of them. However, even if we cannot say that there is a single right answer we can say that there are three approaches to deciding on sample size that are inadequate: Specifiying a fraction of the population to be included in the sample is never the right way to decide on a sample size. Saying that a particular sample size is the usual or typical approach to studying a population is also virtually always the wrong answer. Finally, it is very rare that calculating a desired confidence interval for one variable for an entire population is the best way to decide how big a sample should be.

SAMPLING ERROR AS A COMPONENT
OF TOTAL SURVEY ERROR

The sampling process can affect the quality of survey estimates in three different ways.

If the sample frame excludes some people whom we want to describe, sample estimates will be biased to the extent that those omitted differ from those included.

If the sampling process is not probabilistic, the relationship between the sample and those sampled is problematic. One can argue for the credibility of a sample on grounds other than the sampling process. However, there is no statistical basis for saying a sample is representative of the sampled population unless the sampling process gives each person selected a known probability of selection.

The size and design of a probability sample, together with the distribution of what is being estimated, determine the sampling errors—that is, the chance variations that occur because of collecting data about only a sample of a population. Often sampling errors are presented in ways that imply they are the only source of unreliability in survey estimates. In fact with large samples, other sources of error are likely to be more important. A main theme of this book is that nonsampling errors warrant as much attention as sampling errors. Also it is not uncommon to see sampling errors reported that assume simple random sampling procedures when the sample design involved clusters, or even when it was not a probability sample at all. In these ways, ironically, estimates of sampling errors can mislead readers about the precision or accuracy of sample estimates.

The three main concluding points to be made about sampling errors then are as follows:

(1) Make sure the calculation of sampling errors is appropriate to the sample design.
(2) Consider all sources of error, the sample frame, nonresponse, and response errors (all discussed in subsequent chapters) when evaluating the precision of survey estimates.
(3) Although a specialist can be valuable in all phases of the survey process, the many factors that can afffect the representativeness of a sample and its precision make it virtually essential to involve a sampling specialist both in the design of a sampling plan and in estimating the precision of sample-based estimates.

EXERCISE

In order to grasp the meaning of sampling error, repeated systematic samples of the same size (with different random starts) can be drawn from the same list (e.g., a telephone directory). The proportions of those samples having some characteristic (e.g., a business listing) taken together will form a distribution. That distribution will have a standard deviation that is about one half the entry in Table 2.1 for samples of the sizes drawn.

It is also valuable to calculate several of the entries in Table 2.1 (that is, for various sample sizes and proportions) to help understand how the numbers were derived.

NOTES

1. Different absolute weights can be assigned, but the *product* of the *probability of selection* and the *weight* must be equal for all groups: for example, $1/10 \times 1 = 1/5 \times 1/2$.

2. A systematic sample is usually better, because it would spread selected units around the block.

3

Nonresponse

Implementing a Sample Design

Failure to collect data from a high percentage of those selected to be in a sample is a major source of survey error. Approaches to contacting respondents and enlisting cooperation for mail, telephone, and personal interview surveys are discussed. The biases associated with nonresponse are described, as are the disadvantages of strategies such as quota samples to avoid the effort required to obtain high response rates.

The idea of a probability sample of people is that every individual in the population (or at least the sample frame) has a known chance to have data collected about him or her. A sampling procedure will designate a specific set of individuals (or units of some kind). The quality of sample data depends on the proportion of that set from whom data actually are collected. The procedures used to collect data are as important as the sample selection process in determining how well a sample represents a population.

Of course, in any survey there are some questions that are not answered by all respondents. That rate is low for most questions. Our focus here is on sampled people who do not provide any data at all.

There are three reasons that those selected to be in a sample do not actually provide data:

(a) The data collection procedures do not reach or get to the respondents, thereby not giving them a chance to answer questions.
(b) Those asked to provide data refuse to do so.
(c) Those in the sample asked to provide data are unable to perform the task required of them. For example, some people are too ill to be interviewed, some people do not speak the researcher's language, and, in the case of self-administered questionnaire, some people's reading and writing skills preclude their filling out questionnaires.

The procedures that a researcher decides to use have a major influence on the percentage of a sample that actually provides information (i.e., the response rate) and the extent to which nonrespondents introduce bias into sample data. A critical concern is that in contrast to sampling error, discussed in Chapter 2, the likely effect of nonresponse is to bias samples, that is, to make them systematically different from the population from which they were drawn. In this chapter, we discuss the effect of nonresponse on survey estimates and procedures for reducing nonresponse.

CALCULATING RESPONSE RATES

The response rate is a basic parameter for evaluating a data collection effort. It is simply the number of people interviewed (or responding) divided by the number of people (or units) sampled. The denominator includes all people in the study population who were selected but did not respond for whatever reason: refusals, language problems, illness, or lack of availability.

Sometimes a sample design will involve "screening" to find members of a population to be studied. Screened units that are not in the study population do not enter the response rate calculation. Hence vacant houses, telephone numbers that are not working or that do not serve nonresidential units, and households where no eligible person resides (e.g., households in which no elderly people live when one is drawing a sample of elderly persons) are omitted in calculating response rates. If there are some units for which information needed to determine eligibility is not obtained, however, the response rate is uncertain. The best approach in this situation is to calculate the response rates using conservative and liberal assumptions about the rate of eligibility of unscreened units and report the range, together with a best estimate.

Example. The goal is to select a sample of adults 65 or older by drawing a sample of housing units.

EXAMPLE OF DATA COLLECTION RESULTS

Housing units selected	1200
Not occupied	100

Occupied housing units	1100
Screening not complete	100
Screening complete	1000
Screening results	
No elderly person in home	800
Elderly person in home	200
Interview results for known eligibles	
Interviews completed	150
Refusals	25
Too ill (in hospital)	5
Does not speak English	7
Not at home after six calls	5
Senile	3
Other	5
	200

For households known to include elderly (200), response rate was

$$\frac{150}{200} = .75$$

If all unscreened households (100) included elderly, response rate was

$$\frac{150}{300} = .50$$

A best estimate may be to assume that the unscreened households (100) included elderly at the same rate as screened households (20 percent) in which case the response rate was

$$\frac{150}{220} = .68$$

The response rate for completing the screening process was

$$\frac{1000}{1100} = .91$$

A further calculation can sometimes be made: the fraction of the population represented in the sample. If the sample frame did not omit anyone in the study population, the response rate is the fraction of the population represented in the sample. However, if the above study was a telephone sample and only 95 percent of the elderly had telephones, .95 × .68 (best estimate of response rate) = .65, which is the best estimate of the fraction of the elderly population represented in the sample.

BIAS ASSOCIATED WITH NONRESPONSE

The effect of nonresponse on survey estimates depends on the percentage not responding and the extent to which those not responding are biased—that is, systematically different from the whole population. If most of those selected provide data, sample estimates will be very good even if the nonrespondents are distinctive. For example, when the Bureau of the Census carries out the National Health Interview Survey, it is successful in completing interviews in nearly 95 percent of selected households. It is easy to show that even if the nonresponding 5 percent is very distinctive, the resulting samples are still very similar to the population as a whole.

The experience of the Bureau of the Census is extreme in the positive direction. At the other extreme, one occasionally will see reports of mail surveys in which 5 to 20 percent of the sample responded. In such instances, the final sample has little relationship to the original sampling process. Those responding are essentially self-selected. It is very unlikely that such procedures will provide any credible statistics about the characteristics of the population as a whole.

Most survey research projects lie somewhere between those two extremes. The response rates that even careful organizations achieve depend on many things. Response rates generally are higher in rural areas than they are in central cities. It is easier to collect information from any responsible adult in a household than to obtain an interview with a designated respondent. Some subjects such as health may interest more people than other topics such as economic behavior or public opinions. Moreover, survey organizations differ considerably in the extent to which they devote time and money to improving response rates.

There is no agreed-upon standard for a minimum acceptable response rate. The Office of Management and Budget of the federal government, which reviews surveys done under contract to the government, generally asks that procedures be likely to yield a response rate in excess of 75 percent. Academic survey organizations usually are able to achieve response rates with designated adults in the 75 percent range with general household samples. Rates of response for surveys of central city samples or using random-digit dial telephone samples are distinctively likely to be lower.

The nature of bias associated with nonresponse differs somewhat to mail, telephone, and personal interview procedures. For mail surveys, bias due to nonresponse can be studied by comparing those who respond immediately with those who respond after follow-up steps are taken. One clear generalization that holds up for most mail surveys is that people who have a particular interest in the subject matter or the research itself are more likely to return mail questionnaires than those who are less interested. This means that mail surveys with low response rates almost invariably will be biased significantly in ways that are related directly to the purposes of the research (Donald, 1960).

An example of significant bias from low response to mail questionnaires is the oft-cited *Literary Digest* presidential poll in 1936. It has been told frequently that the *Literary Digest* managed to predict a strong victory for Alf Landon, an election that Franklin Roosevelt won by a political landslide. Somehow, the story has been passed on in some statistical texts that the failure lay in the sample frame. Specifically, it is told that a sample was drawn from telephone books, and Republicans, which Landon was, were more likely to have telephones in 1936. However, it turns out that story is incorrect. In fact, the *Literary Digest* survey in 1936 was a mail survey. Its failure was one of nonresponse. Only a minority of those asked to return questionnaires did so. As is typical of mail surveys, those who wanted the underdog to win were particularly likely to want to express their views (Bryson, 1976).

Virtually every study of the patterns of return of self-administered questionnaires shows that early returns are biased. It is important to realize that samples of data resulting from returns of 20 or 30 percent, which are not uncommon for mail surveys that are not followed up effectively, usually look nothing at all like the sampled populations.

The other consistent bias in mail surveys is that better-educated people usually send back mail questionnaires more quickly than those with less education. Therefore, any mail study of any variable that is likely to be related to education (which is, in turn, related to income level) likely will produce biased estimates unless steps are taken to achieve high response rates.

The biases associated with telephone and personal household interview surveys are somewhat different. In these surveys, respondent interest is probably a less important factor in nonresponse than with mail surveys. Interviewers talking with people face to face or on the telephone are more effective at presenting a research project to respondents than a letter in the mail. Subject matter, however, does have some bearing on nonresponse. For example, studies of political attitudes and public opinions tend to produce disproportionate nonresponse among less-educated people. The likely reason is that education is related to interest and knowledge about such topics. On the other hand, it appears that people with high incomes have some tendency to avoid studies of income and economic behavior. Presumably, income is a more sensitive topic for people with high incomes.

Availability is a more important source of nonresponse for telephone and personal surveys than for mail surveys. It is obvious that if a data collection effort is carried out between and 9:00 and 5:00 Mondays through Fridays, the people who will be available to be interviewed will be distinctive. Since those who are home will tend not to have jobs, the survey is likely to yield high proportions of housewives and mothers, unemployed persons, and retired people. They will tend not to have busy volunteer and social lives. They are more likely to be parents of small children. Large households are more likely to have someone at home than households with only one or two people.

Accessibility of a different kind also produces biases associated with nonresponse. National surveys using personal interview procedures almost always have lower response rates in central cities than in the suburbs and rural areas. There are three main reasons for this. First, the rate of hard-to-find single individuals is higher in central cities. Second, an increasing fraction of individuals in central cities live in high-rise apartment buildings, where interviewers have difficulty gaining direct access to people. Third, there are more areas in central cities where visits at night are uncomfortable for interviewers. Hence, they may not give difficult-to-find people as good a chance to be found at home. Marquis (1978) presents a good summary of national trends in nonresponse.

There is some evidence that telephone procedures may reduce the differential response rate between central cities and rural areas because it is possible to give thorough coverage to urban households, to make contact with people in high-security buildings, and to make a very large number of efforts to find single people at home.

Another common nonresponse bias is that less-educated people seem less willing to be interviewed in a random-digit dial telephone procedure. That same bias also prevails among the elderly and any other group where the level of education is lower than average. That bias is found less often in personal interview surveys.

Finally, there is bias associated with people who are unable to be interviewed or to fill out a form. That usually is a small fraction of a general population. However, leaving out people who are in a hospital

TABLE 3.1
Effect of Biased Nonresponse on Survey Estimates

Response Rate (%)	Percentage of Nonrespondents with Characteristic						
	10	20	25	30	40	50	75
90	27	26	25	24	23	22	19
80	28	26	25	24	21	19	13
70	31	27	25	23	19	14	3
60	35	28	25	22	15	8	
50	40	30	25	20	10		
40	47	33	25	17			
30	60	37	25	13			

NOTE: Estimate calculated from sample when true population rate is 25%.

may be a very important omission when trying to estimate health care utilization or expenditures. There are neighborhood areas or groups where omitting people who do not speak English would be a serious omission. If special steps are not taken to collect data from a particular group, the sample estimates apply to a more restricted population: the population that actually had a chance to answer the questions or provide data, given the field procedures implemented.

Table 3.1 is an effort to put together information about the response rate and the extent of bias among nonrespondents to provide some indication of the likely impact on data. The table uses, as an example, estimates from a sample when the actual rate of some characteristic in the population is 25 percent. It considers various degrees of nonresponse bias: a little bias (when 20 or 30 percent of the nonrespondents have the characteristic), moderate bias (when 10 or 40 percent of the nonrespondents have the characteristic), and significant bias (when 50 or 75 percent of the nonrespondents have the characteristics to be estimated).

If nonresponse is not biased (i.e., when the rate of the characteristic is 25 percent among nonrespondents), the response rate does not affect estimates. However, when there are major biases in the characteristics of nonrespondents, even studies with response rates in the 70 to 80 percent range produce considerable error. When response rates are lower—60 percent and below—estimates are not very good even when bias is modest.

It may be instructive to compare the effects of nonresponse bias, such as those presented in Table 3.1, with the effects of sampling error presented in the preceding chapter (Table 2.1). We usually do not know how biased nonresponse is, but it is seldom a good assumption that nonresponse is unbiased. Clearly therefore, efforts to ensure that response rates reach a reasonable level and to avoid procedures that systematically produce major differences between respondents and nonrespondents should be a standard part of any survey effort.

REDUCING NONRESPONSE IN TELEPHONE OR
PERSONAL INTERVIEW SURVEYS

Just as one can always say that a larger sample will be more reliable than a small sample, all other things being equal, one also can say that a higher response rate will produce a better and less biased sample than one that has more nonresponse.[1] As with any design decision, a researcher must choose how much effort to invest in reducing nonresponse.

Two different problems must be addressed in order to achieve a high rate of response for a telephone and personal surveys. One must gain access to the selected individuals and one must enlist cooperation.

In order to reduce nonresponse due to lack of availability,

(1) Make numerous calls, concentrating on evenings and weekends. The number needed depends on the setting. Typically, six calls per household are probably a minimum in urban areas. For phone studies, more calls can be made cheaply, and many organizations use ten as a minimum.

(2) Have interviewers with flexible schedules who can make appointments at any time that is convenient to respondents.

To enlist cooperation,

(1) If possible, send an informative advance letter. It reassures some respondents, and interviewers feel more confident, too.

(2) Effectively and accurately present the purposes of the project. Make sure respondents know their help is important and how it will be useful.

(3) Make sure that respondents will not be threatened by the task or the uses to which the data will be put.

(4) Have effective interviewers. Make sure they know that the response rate is important. Identify response rate problems quickly and either retrain or do not continue to use interviewers who are not effective.

The interview process is generally a positive experience for respondents. If a survey research project is being conducted by a responsible group, responses will be kept strictly confidential. Survey researchers routinely respect confidentiality with the same zealousness that psychiatrists and journalists protect their sources. Most survey research projects are serving some reasonable cause to which the majority of people would be willing to contribute. If the interviewer is willing to arrange an interview at the respondent's convenience, pressures for time should not be extraordinary for most respondents. Finally, most respondents report that being interviewed is pleasurable. People like to have an opportunity to talk about themselves to a good listener.

The effectiveness of these procedures in countering problems of access and cooperation will vary from study to study for reasons noted above. In general, however, if response rates are much below 65 percent, it generally means that one or more of the basic steps outlined above was missing.

REDUCING NONRESPONSE TO MAIL SURVEYS

The problems of reducing nonresponse to mail surveys are somewhat different. Getting to the respondent, which is a critical part of telephone and personal surveys, is generally not an issue if the researcher has an accurate mailing address. Most people eventually come home to pick up their mail. Rather, the main difficulty is inducing respondents to perform the task of filling out the questionnaire without the intervention of an interviewer.

Writing a letter is not a very effective way to convince a high percentage of people to do something. Personal contact is significantly more effective than a letter. There is a large literature on strategies designed to attempt to make a mail contact more effective. Does one print a questionnaire on colored paper or white paper? How much good does an impressive letterhead do? How about endorsements? What is the value of paying people? Some researchers send money along with the questionnaire, while others promise reimbursement if the questionnaire is returned. Should the respondent letter be signed in blue ink? Is a real stamp better than a postage-paid envelope?

Generally speaking, almost anything that makes a mail questionnaire look more professional, more personalized, or more attractive will have some positive effect on response rates. Tending to such details probably is worthwhile in the aggregate (Linsky, 1975, reviews these issues well).

It probably is also important to make the instrument easy to complete. More details about design are provided in Chapter 6, but there are three points worth mentioning here.

(1) The task should be clear.
(2) The questions should be attractively spaced, easy to read, and uncluttered.
(3) The response task itself should be easy. Do not ask respondents to provide written answers, except at their option. The response task should be to check a box or circle a number or some other equally simple task.

While attractive presentation of the study and good questionnaire design all help, there is no question that the most important difference between good mail surveys and poor mail surveys is the extent to which researchers make repeated contact with nonrespondents. A reasonable sequence of events might include the following:

(1) About ten days after the initial mailing, mail all nonrespondents a reminder card, emphasizing the importance of the study and of a high rate of response.
(2) About ten days after the postcard is mailed, mail the remaining nonrespondents a letter again emphasizing the importance of a high rate of return and including another questionnaire for those who threw the first one away.
(3) If the response rate is still not satisfactory, probably the best next step is to call nonrespondents on the telephone. If phone numbers are not available or if the expense of personal calls seems too great, additional persuasion letters, night telegraph letters, or other follow-up procedures that stand out and seem important have been shown to be helpful.

The difficulties of getting the response rate to a reasonable level will depend on the nature of the sample, the nature of the study, how motivated people are, and how easy the task is for them. Clearly, the task will be easier if the sample is composed of motivated, well-educated individuals. However, Dillman has obtained response rates over 70 percent with general population samples, using only mail procedures (Dillman et al., 1974). Hochstim (1967) obtained response rates over 80 percent with telephone and personal follow-ups. If the researcher will be persistent, and if it is a reasonably well-conceived and well-designed study, acceptable response rates can be obtained by mail.

If a researcher is going to follow up nonrespondents, the researcher must know who has not returned a questionnaire. The process need not be circuitious or complex. A simple identifying number can be written on the questionnaire or on the return envelope. It is good practice to tell people in the covering letter what the number is for.

Occasionally, a researcher may want to reassure respondents that they will not be identified. There is a simple alternative strategy that works very well and still permits follow-up. The respondent is sent a questionnaire that has no identifier on it. Attached to the questionnaire is a separate postcard that has a respondent identifier, as follows:

> Dear Researcher, I am sending this postcard at the same time that I am putting my completed questionnaire in the mail. Since my questionnaire is completely anonymous, this postcard will tell you that you need not send me a further reminder to participate in your study.

This procedure maintains the respondent's anonymity, at the same time telling the researcher when someone has completed the questionnaire. Someone might think that respondents simply would send back the postcard in order to avoid further reminders. That seldom happens. The number of postcards and questionnaires returned almost always comes out to be about the same.

NONPROBABILITY
(OR MODIFIED PROBABILITY) SAMPLES

The discussion in this chapter so far has assumed a probability sample design, whereby respondents are designated by some objective procedure. The researcher's problem is to collect data about those designated. There is, however, a commonly used selection approach (or set of approaches) that does not designate specific individuals and for which response rates cannot be calculated. The reason such nonprobability samples are discussed here is that, in essence, nonprobability samples are comparable to samples that result from very low response rates—except the response rates are not calculable, and hence users may not know the limits of the data they are using.

The disagreement among survey researchers about the importance of probability sampling is intriguing. The federal government generally will not fund survey research efforts designed to make estimates of population characteristics that are not based on probability sampling techniques. Most academic survey organizations and many nonprofit research organizations have a similar approach to sampling. At the same time, almost all of the major public opinion polling groups, political polling groups, and market research organizations rely solely on nonprobability sampling methods.

The heart of probability sampling strategies is that the inclusion of someone in a sample is based purely on a predetermined procedure that sets a rate of selection for defined population subgroups. Beyond that, neither respondent characteristics nor interviewer discretion influence the likelihood that a person will be in a sample. Although nonprobability modifications of sampling procedures vary, they all share the property that, at the last stage, interviewer discretion and/or respondent characteristics not part of the sample design affect the likelihood of being included in a sample. Let us describe the two most common procedures.

For a personal interview study involving nonprobabilistic sampling, the researchers might draw blocks in much the same way that a sampler would draw blocks for an area probability sample. The difference would be that once a block was selected, the interviewer would be instructed to visit that block and complete six (or some fixed number of) interviews with people who reside on the block. There would be no specific listing of housing units on the block. The interviewer would be free to call on any home located on that block; the interviewer would not make callbacks to find people not at home.

A similar strategy is used for telephone surveys. Within a particular exchange, an interviewer is given a list of random numbers from which to complete a certain number of interviews. If there is no answer or no available respondent at the time the interviewer calls, another number is called.

The first stage of sampling, if it is carried out as indicated above, distributes the sample around a geographic area more or less in the way that the population is distributed. However, at the point of household and respondent selection, there are three very clear kinds of biases that can be introduced.

In the personal interview strategy, but not the telephone strategy, interviewers can make a choice about which houses to visit. It turns out that interviewers will visit more attractive houses rather than less attractive houses. Interviewers prefer first-floor apartments to second- and third-floor apartments. Interviewers prefer housing units without dogs. Other factors that influence choices made by individual interviewers can be left to the reader's imagination.

Some research organizations attempt to restrict interviewer discretion by providing instructions about where on the block to start and asking interviewers not to skip housing units. However, without an advance listing of what is on the block, it is virtually impossible to supervise whether or not an interviewer carried out those instructions. On the other hand, if there is an advance listing of units on the street, one portion of the cost savings of this approach is eliminated.

The second biasing feature of the nonprobability methods is the effect of availability. If one is not going to call back to the housing units where no one is home, the housing units where people are home have a much higher chance of being selected than housing units where people routinely are not at home. Women, people who are not employed, parents of children, and the other biases discussed above all are related to availability.

Uncontrolled sampling in this way produces some obvious sample biases. The most common approach to increasing the quality of the samples is to introduce quotas for obvious biases. Thus an interviewer may be required to interview half males and half females from any particular block or telephone cluster. Occasionally, some additional constraints will be set such as the expected racial composition or the number of old or young adults. However, it is important not to put too many constraints on the quotas or interviewers will have to spend a great deal of time calling or wandering around blocks looking for eligible respondents.

The final bias inherent in quota or nonprobability samples has to do with the enlistment of cooperation. In the event that a respondent says that he or she is busy or it is not a good time to be interviewed, the interviewer has no incentive to enlist cooperation. If a project is not effectively presented, a significant fraction of the population will not be interested in helping. Letting people easily refuse without strenuous effort to present the study to them will not only bias a sample against the busy people but also will bias it against the people who

have less prior knowledge or less intrinsic interest in research and/or
in the particular subject matter being studied.

Sudman (1967, 1976) argues that there is nonresponse in all surveys, even those in which every effort is made to contact nonrespondents. Once it has been learned that an individual will not cooperate
or cannot be reached after several calls, he suggests that substituting a
respondent from the same block actually may improve the quality of
estimates. He argues that having a neighbor in the sample may be
better than having neither the designated respondent nor his neighbor
in the sample. When careful control is exercised over the interviewers' discretion, however, as Sudman advocates, the savings in reduced callbacks are offset largely by increased supervisory costs.

Nonprobability sampling methods produce cost savings for personal interview surveys, less so for telephone surveys. Moreover, the
resulting samples often look rather similar to probability sample data,
to the extent that they can be compared. However, two facts should
be kept in mind.

First, because the key to saving money is to make no callbacks,
only about a third of the population has a chance to be in most
nonprobability sample polls (i.e., the population that is at home on a
typical first call). A sample that only gives a third of the population a
chance to be selected, that is, a third of the population with known
distinctive characteristics, has great potential to be atypical in ways
that will affect sample statistics.

Second, the assumptions of probability theory and sampling error,
which routinely are touted as describing the reliability of nonprobability samples, do not apply. If there are substitutes, the sample is not a
probability sample, though it may be spread around the population in
a reasonably realistic way.

If a researcher decides to use a nonprobability sample, readers
should be told how the sample was drawn, the fact that it likely is
biased in the direction of availability and willingness to be interviewed, and that the normal assumptions for calculating sampling
errors do not apply. Such warnings to readers are not common. In
many cases, nonprobability samples are misrepresented seriously and
their use constitutes a serious problem for the credibility of social
science research.

NONRESPONSE AS A SOURCE OF ERROR
IN SURVEY SAMPLES

Nonresponse is a problematic, important source of error in surveys. What we know suggests it is potentially quite biasing. Yet

although we can calculate a rate of response, we usually do not know the effect of nonresponse on the data because it is hard to learn much about nonrespondents.

When data collection procedures produce returns from only a minority of selected samples, the results seldom look similar to the population as a whole; it is hard to make a credible case that such samples are probably representative. However, even surveys that are done with reasonable care can generate response rates in the sixties and low seventies. As we have seen, when nonresponse is in that range, it can have a notable effect on sample estimates even if the nonresponse is biased only modestly.

Of course, nonresponse is not always very biased; but it usually is. Availability typically is associated with age, being married, and being employed. Refusals to mail questionnaires almost always are biased toward education and interest. Nonresponse in telephone surveys usually is biased with respect to age and education.

Response rates are largely under the control of the researcher. Presenting the study effectively and effort to enlist cooperation make a major difference. For most surveys, nonresponse is potentially one of the most important sources of systematic error; it is likely to be one of the most problematic concerns regarding the accuracy of sample estimates. Hence attention to minimizing its effects deserves very high priority in the total design of surveys.

EXERCISE

If a sample of households is selected as the first stage of sampling adults aged 18 or older in Middletown, the response rate is the number of completed interviews divided by the number of individuals in the study population designated by the sampling procedure to be in the sample. Would you include or exclude the following groups from the denominator when calculating the response rate? (Why?)

Vacant housing units
Those who were away on vacation
Those temporarily in the hospital
Those who refused to be interviewed
Housing units in which all residents were under 18
Those who could not speak the researcher's language
Those whom others in the households said were mentally ill or too
    confused to be interviewed
Those who were never at home when the interviewer called
Those who were away at college

Define the population to whom your sample statistics (and your response rate) apply.

NOTE

1. It is true that if reluctant respondents are induced to answer questions, the poor quality of their reporting may produce more error than their inclusion in the sample avoids.

4

Methods of Data Collection

The choice of data collection mode—mail, telephone, personal interview, or group administration—is related directly to the sample frame, research topic, characteristics of the sample, and available staff and facilities; it has implications for response rates, question form, and survey costs. An inventory of the various considerations in and consequences of the choice of a data collection mode is presented in this chapter.

One of the most far-reaching decisions a researcher must make is the way in which the data will be collected. Should an interviewer ask the questions and record the answers, or should the survey be self-administered? If an interviewer is to be used, there is the further decision about whether the interview will take place in person or over the telephone. If the respondent is to read and answer questions without an interviewer, there are choices about how to present the questionnaire to the respondents. In some cases, questionnaires are handed to respondents, in groups or individually, and returned immediately. In households surveys, questionnaires can be dropped off at a home or mailed and returned in a similiar fashion.

Although the majority of surveys utilize a single data collection method, it is not uncommon for combinations of methods to be used. For example, personal interview surveys sometimes have sections of questions that respondents answer by filling out a self-administered form. To reduce nonresponse, people who fail to return mail questionnaires sometimes are contacted by an interviewer on the phone or in person. Respondents whom personal interviewers are unable to find at home or who have moved out of an area may be interviewed by telephone or asked to complete a self-administered form. Finally, some household surveys utilize telephone interviews to interview people at addresses for which telephone numbers can be obtained, but use a personal interviewer in households for which no telephone number can be found.

There are conditions under which each of these approaches to data collection is the best. In this chapter, our goal is to *discuss the bases on which to choose among the various data collection approaches.*

MAJOR ISSUES IN CHOOSING A STRATEGY

Sampling

The way a researcher plans to draw a sample is related to the best way to collect data. Certain kinds of sampling approaches make it easy or difficult to use one or another data collection strategy.

If one is sampling from a list, the information on the list matters. Obviously, if a list lacks either a good mailing address or a good telephone number, trying to collect data either by mail or phone is complicated.

Random-digit dialing has improved the potential of telephone data collection strategies by giving every household with a telephone a chance of being selected. Assuming one is willing to omit those without telephones, it is perhaps the least expensive way to draw a general household sample.

Of course, it is possible to use random-digit dialing strategies simply to sample and make initial contact with households, followed by data collection through the use of some other mode. Once a household has been reached, one can ask for an address to permit either a mail questionnaire to be sent or an interviewer to visit. Such designs are particularly useful when one is looking for a rare population, since both the sampling and the screening via telephone are comparatively less expensive than doing the same task with a personal interviewer. The difficulty with such strategies may lie in the rate of cooperation at the time of data collection.

When the basis of the sample is a set of addresses, either from a list or from an area probability sample, telephone, personal interview, and mail procedures all may be feasible. Obviously, if one has a good address, one can send an interviewer. In addition, it is possible to obtain telephone numbers for many addresses. For example, in most central cities there is a city directory that lists telephone numbers for a reasonable fraction of households by address. In some cities, research organizations can gain access to a reverse telephone directory, in which published telephone numbers are listed by address. Finally, if field listing is used in sampling, interviewers can make an effort to get names when they list addresses. It then is possible to obtain telephone numbers in regular telephone directories.

Such approaches will not produce telephone numbers for all addresses. Therefore, some other mode of data collection will be needed as a supplement. However, it often is possible to interview a majority by telephone, thereby realizing the potential advantages of that mode.

If one samples from a good list of addresses, a mail survey also is feasible. However, in an urban area with many multiunit dwellings, it is important that there be apartment unit designations (or household names) as well as a street address. Without an apartment unit or name, a mailing to a multiunit structure will go undelivered, or will not reach the right unit.

The problem is equally troublesome in rural areas where there are no specific addresses associated with housing units. Therefore, if a rural sample frame does not include names, a mail survey is out of the question.

A final sampling issue to consider is designating a respondent. If the sample frame is a list of individuals, any procedure including mail is feasible. However, many surveys entail designating a specific respondent at the time of data collection. If a questionnaire is mailed to a household or organization, the researcher has little control over who actually completes the questionnaire. Therefore, the involvement of an interviewer is a critical aid if respondent designation is an issue.

Type of Population

The reading and writing skills of the population and their motivation to cooperate are two salient considerations in choosing a mode of data collection.

Self-administered approaches to data collection place more of a burden on the reading and writing skills of the respondent than do interviewer procedures. Respondents who are not very well educated, whose reading and writing skills in English are less than facile (but who can speak English), people who do not see well, and people who are somewhat ill or tire easily all will find an interviewer-administered survey easier than filling out a self-administered form.

Another problem for mail surveys is getting people to return a completed questionnaire. We know that people who are particularly interested in the research problem will be most likely to return questionnaires.

In this context, if one is collecting data from a population that is highly literate and that, on the average, is likely to be highly interested in the research, mail procedures become more attractive. At the other extreme, if one is dealing with population for which reading and writing skills are likely to be low and/or where the average level of interest and motivation is estimated to be low, interviewer-administered data collection strategies are likely to be preferable.

Question Form

Generally speaking, if one is going to have a self-administered questionnaire, one must reconcile oneself to closed questions—that is, questions that can be answered by simply checking a box or circling the proper response from a set provided by the researcher. There are two reasons for this. First, asking people to answer questions in their own words increases the difficulty of their task, which will affect the rate of nonresponse for many types of respondents. Second, and more important, self-administered open answers often do not produce useful data. With no interviewer present to probe incomplete answers for clarity and for meeting consistent question objectives, the answers will not be comparable across respondents, and they will be difficult to code. If such answers are useful at all, it usually is when they are treated as annecdotal material, not as measures.

While open questions usually require an interviewer, there are also some instances where closed questions can be handled better by self—administered procedures. One very good example is when a researcher wants to ask a large number of items that are in a similar form. Having an interviewer read long lists of similar items can be awkward. On such occasions, a good strategy may be to put the questions in a self-administered questionnaire. Such an approach also provides a welcome change of pace for an interview.

Self-administered procedures also have an advantage when question response categories are numerous or complex. In a personal interview, it is common to hand the respondent a card listing responses to help respondents keep all the possible answers in mind. However, telephone surveys require some adjustments. Three approaches are used.

First, researchers simply may limit response scales for telephone interviews. Some have argued that four categories is a comfortable maximum on the telephone; for many telephone surveys, two- or three-category responses predominate.

Second, a longer list can be handled if a telephone interviewer reads the categories slowly, then reads them again, with the respondent choosing the correct category when the interviewer gets to it. It has not been demonstrated, however, that answers obtained in this way are identical to those given to a visual list of categories. For some kinds of questions, the answers are affected by the order in which responses are read (Schuman & Presser, 1981).

Third, researchers can break down complex questions into a set of two or more simpler questions. For example, it is common to ask people to report their income in more than four or five categories. A nine-category question can be asked in two phases as follows: "Would you say that your total family income is less than $15,000, between $15,000 and $30,000, or over $30,000?" Then, depending on the answer, the interviewer proceeds to ask another three-alternative question such as: "Well, would you say that your total family income was less than $20,000 $20,000 to $25,000, or over $25,000?"

There are question forms, including those with complex descriptions of situations or events and those requiring pictures or other visual cues, that cannot be adapted to the telephone. If such measurement is a critical part of a survey, some form other than the telephone probably is needed. However, researchers have shown that they can adapt the majority of survey questions to telephone use.

Question Content

In the last 20 years, several studies have compared the results of different data collection strategies (e.g., Hochstim, 1967; Klecka &Tuchfarber, 1978; Groves & Kahn, 1979; Mangione et al., 1982; Colombotos, 1969). For most survey questions studied, the aggregate distributions obtained by personal interview, telephone interview, and self-administered procedures have been indistinguishable. Moreover, many potentially sensitive subjects such as alcohol use and family planning techniques have been studied using telephone survey procedures.

Researchers have argued persuasively that one or another of the strategies should have an advantage when dealing with sensitive topics. Self-administered procedures are thought to be best because the respondent does not have to admit directly to an interviewer a socially undesirable or negatively valued characteristic or behavior. Others have argued that telephone procedures lend an air of impersonality to the interview process that should help people report negative events or behaviors. Moreover, random-digit dialing at least provides the option of having a virtually anonymous survey procedure, since the interviewer need not know the name or location of the respondent. Still others argue that personal interviewers are the best way to ask sensitive questions. Interviewers have an opportunity to build rapport and to establish the kind of trust that is needed for respondents to report potentially sensitive information.

While all these arguments sound plausible, findings have been somewhat inconsistent (see Singer, 1981). The following generalizations are probably accurate. First, it is very unusual for self-administered forms to not be at least as good as the other methods at eliciting responses that may be socially sensitive or embarrassing. Second, it is probably most common for a telephone procedure to show differences in the direction suggesting a social desirability bias. One of the most striking such differences was found by Mangione et al. (1982) in the rate at which people admitted having past drinking problems. Telephone procedures proved to elicit much lower rates of such reports than either personal interview or self-administered procedures Hochstim (1967) and Hensen et al. (1977) found consistent results. Third, if very sensitive material is involved, most researchers would want at least an initial personal contact with the respondent, though self-administered questions and later telephone reinterviews might be part of the overall design.

An entirely different aspect of question content that may affect the mode of data collection is the difficulty of the reporting task. In some surveys, researchers want to ask about events or behaviors that are difficult to report with accuracy because they extend over a period of time or are quite detailed. In such cases, reporting accuracy may benefit from a chance to consult records or to discuss the questions with other family members. The standard interview is a quick question-and-answer process that provides little such opportunity; that is especially true for telephone interviews. Self-administered procedures provide more time for thought, for checking records, and for consulting with other family members.

Overall, when samples are comparable, researchers have found that most survey estimates are unaffected by the mode of data collection. Unless some of the issues outlined above are very central to the research project, it is likely that the decision about how to collect data should be made on grounds other than the interaction between the subject matter of the questionnaire and the mode of data collection.

Response Rates

The rate of response is likely to be much more salient in the selection of a data collection procedure than other considerations.

Obviously, one of the great strengths of group-administered surveys, when they are feasible, is the high rate of response. Generally speaking, when students in classrooms or workers at job settings are asked to complete questionnaires, the rate of response is near 100 percent. The limits on response usually stem from absenteeism or scheduling (shifts, days off).

There is no doubt that the problem of nonresponse is central to the use of mail surveys. As noted in the previous chapter, if one simply mails questionnaires to a general population sample without appropriate follow-up procedures, the rate of return is likely to be less than 30 percent. With virtually all populations, without follow-up procedures only a minority of potential respondents will return a questionnaire. If extensive and appropriate follow-up procedures are utilized and if the project is otherwise well designed and executed, response rates can be obtained for mail surveys similar to rates obtained using other modes (e.g., Dillman et al., 1974). However, obtaining an adequate rate of response is a special challenge of mail procedures.

The effectiveness of telephone strategies to produce high response rates depends on the sampling scheme. One way of utilizing the telephone for surveys is to replicate personal interview procedures. If one has a list of addresses as well as telephone numbers, an advance letter can be mailed introducing the study and explaining the purposes. After that, an interviewer can call on the telephone and ask for cooperation. Under those circumstances, telephone and personal response rates do not differ significantly. This is particularly true if interviewers can offer the option to nonrespondents to being interviewed in person (Hochstim, 1967; Mangione et al., 1982).

The procedures outlined above, however, are representative of only a minority of telephone surveys. Much more common are studies where the telephone is linked with random-digit dialing sampling. One distinctive characteristic of random-digit dialing is that no advance notice to respondents is possible, since addresses are not known. Competent and conscientious survey organizations report response rates more than five percentage points lower than those they obtain by personal interview (e.g., Groves & Kahn, 1979).

Response rates in some urban areas benefit from using the telephone, while suburban and rural rates are usually lower on the telephone than when a personal interviewer is used. Using the telephone permits better coverage of units in buildings with security systems and neighborhoods where interviewers are reluctant to go in the evenings. Also in a telephone survey, 10 or even 15 callbacks can be made to find a respondent who is seldom home. On the other hand, as noted in Chapter 3, there is distinctive nonresponse associated with education and age in random-digit dialed telephone surveys that is less apparent in personal interview surveys.

In conclusion, when advance letters are possible, there is no difference between telephone and personal interview procedures with respect to response. Moreover, when researchers want to reinterview people previously interviewed to get further information, the rate of response via the telephone is no different from that obtained by personal interviewers. For studies of some central city populations, telephone strategies, even utilizing random-digit dialing, probably can produce response rates that are nearly as good as, occasionally even better than, those that will be obtained by personal interview procedures.

For broader populations, it appears that one of the costs of random-digit dialing telephone surveys is that the rate of response of selected households is lower than will be obtained by the personal interview survey. When a five to ten percentage point reduction in response rates is multiplied by the rate at which people without phones also are omitted from such samples, the differential in the rate of response is not trivial. That is a disadvantage that researchers must be prepared to accept, or to work very hard to avoid, when they choose a random-digit dial approach.

Costs

The great appeal of mail and telephone survey procedures is that they cost less in most cases than personal interviews. Survey costs depend on a multitude of factors. Some of the more salient factors are the amount of professional time required to design the questionnaire, the questionnaire length, the geographic dispersion of the sample, the availability and interest of the sample, the callback procedures, respondent selection rules, and the availability of trained staff.

Although on the surface mail survey costs might appear to be lowest, the cost of postage, of clerical time for mailing, and of printing questionnaires turns out not to be trivial. Moreover, if there are telephone follow-ups, the expense gets higher. In general, properly executed mail surveys are likely to be very similar in cost to telephone surveys. One key to the comparison may include the telephone charges that are involved.

Telephone use costs also will affect the personal-telephone cost comparison, but personal household interviews almost always will cost more than telephone interviews with the same sample. Necessarily, the wages and expenses for an interviewer to visit a house and make contact with a respondent will exceed those for telephoning.

While the choice between mail and telephone surveys often can be made on grounds unrelated to cost, cost usually has to play a role in choosing a personal interview procedure. Yet there are many cases in which the strengths of the personal interview procedure make it the best choice to achieve a given set of research objectives.

Available Facilities

The facilities and staff available should be considered in choosing a data collection mode. The development of an interviewing staff is costly and difficult. Attrition rates are generally high for newly trained interviewers. Many new interviewers are not very good at enlisting cooperation of respondents, producing high refusal rates at the start. In addition, people who are good at training and surpervising interviewers are not easy to find. Thus one very practical consideration for anyone thinking about doing an interviewer-conducted survey is the ability to execute a professional data collection effort. If one has access to an ongoing survey operation or if staff members have experience in interviewer supervision and training, interviewer studies become more feasible. If not, self-administered surveys have a real advantage.

Length of Data Collection

The time involved in the data collection varies by mode. Mail surveys usually take two months to complete. A normal sequence involves mailing the questionnaires, waiting for a while, doing some more mailing, some more waiting, and some eventual follow-up.

At the other extreme, it is quite feasible to do telephone surveys in a few days. The very quickest surveys pay a cost in nonresponse, since some people cannot be reached during any short period. However, telephone surveys routinely can be done more quickly than a mail or personal interview survey of comparable size.

The length of time required to do a personal interview survey is virtually incalculable, simply because it depends so much on the sample size and the availability of staff. However, it is safe to say that it is only a very unusual circumstance in which the data collection period for personal interviewing would not be greater than for a comparable telephone survey.

SUMMARY COMPARISON

The preceding discussion is not exhaustive, but it does cover most of the major considerations. The choice of data collection mode is a complex one that involves many aspects of the survey research process. A summary of most of the strengths and weaknesses of the main approaches to collecting data follows:

Potential advantages of personal interviewing:

(1) There are some sample designs that can be implemented best by personal interview (e.g., area probability samples).
(2) Personal interview procedures are probably the most effective way of enlisting cooperation for most populations.
(3) Advantages of interviewer administration—answering respondent questions, probing for adequate answers, accurately following complex instructions or sequences—are realized.
(4) Multimethod data collection—including observations, visual cues, and self-administered sections—are feasible.
(5) Rapport and confidence building are possible (including any written reassurances that may be needed for reporting very sensitive material).
(6) Probably longer interviews can be done in person.

Potential disadvantages of personal interviewing:

(1) It is likely to be more costly than the alternatives.
(2) A trained staff of interviewers that is geographically near the sample is needed.
(3) Total data collection period is likely to be longer than telephone procedures.
(4) Some samples (those in high-rise buildings or high-crime areas, elites, employees, students) may be more accessible by some other mode.

Potential advantages of telephone interviewing:

(1) Lower costs (compare personal interviews).
(2) Random-digit dialing sampling of general populations.
(3) Access to certain populations (compare especially personal interviews).
(4) Potential for short data collection period.
(5) The advantages of interviewer administration (compare mail).
(6) Interviewer staffing and management easier (compare personal interviews)—smaller staff needed, need not be near sample, supervision and quality control potentially better.
(7) Likely better response rate from a list sample (compare mail only).

Potential disadvantages of telephone studies:

(1) Sampling limitations, especially problem of omitting those without telephones.
(2) Nonresponse associated with RDD sampling (compare personal).

(3) Questionnaire or measurement constraints, including limits on response alternatives, impossibility of visual aids, and interviewer observations.

(4) Possibly less appropriate for personal or sensitive questions if no prior contact.

Potential advantages of self-administered (compare interviewer-administered) data collections:

(1) Ease of presenting questions requiring visual aids (compare telephone).

(2) Asking questions with long or complex response categories.

(3) Asking batteries of similar questions.

(4) The fact that the respondent does not have to share answers with an interviewer.

Potential disadvantages of self-administration:

(1) Especially careful questionnaire design is needed.

(2) Open questions usually are not useful.

(3) Good reading and writing skills by respondents are needed.

(4) The interviewer is not present to exercise quality control with respect to answering all questions, meeting question objectives, or the quality of answers provided.

Self-administered surveys can be done by mail, via group administration, or in households. Each approach has strengths and potential weaknesses.

The advantages of group administration:

(1) Generally high cooperation rates.

(2) The chance to explain the study and answer questions about questionnaire (compare mail).

(3) Generally low cost.

The main disadvantage is that only a small number of surveys can use samples that can be gotten together in a group.

The advantages of mail procedures:

(1) Relatively low cost.

(2) Can be accomplished with minimal staff and facilities.

(3) Provides access to widely dispersed samples and samples that are difficult to reach by telephone or in person for other reasons.

(4) Respondents have time to give thoughtful answers, to look up records, or consult with others.

Disadvantages of mail procedures:

(1) Ineffectiveness of mail as way of enlisting cooperation (depending on group to be studied).

(2) Various disadvantages of not having interviewer involved in data collections.
(3) Need for good mailing addresses for sample.

Dropping off (and later picking up) a questionnaire at a household has advantages:

(1) The interviewer can explain the study, answer questions, and designate a household respondent (compare mail).
(2) Response rates tend to be like those to personal interview studies.
(3) There is opportunity to give thoughtful answers, consult records or other family members (compare personal or telephone).

The disadvantages include the following:

(1) This procedure costs about as much as personal interviews.
(2) A field staff is required (albeit perhaps a less thoroughly trained one than would be needed for personal interviews).

Finally, when considering options, researchers also should consider combinations of modes. As noted, most measures are not affected by mode of data collection. Combinations of personal, telephone, and mail procedures may offer the cost savings associated with the less expensive modes without the sampling or nonresponse prices they sometimes entail.

CONCLUSION

It is clear that the choice of mode is a complex decision and depends very much on the particular study situation. All of the above strategies are the best choice for some studies. However, it is appropriate to note that the pendulum definitely has changed with respect to surveys of general, household-based samples. Twenty years ago, a researcher would assume that a personal interview survey was the method of choice for most studies. The burden of proof would be on the person who would argue that another method could produce data that were as satisfactory.

Now because of the cost advantages, a researcher must address directly the question of why the survey cannot be carried out by telephone. Although mail surveys have their place, in many instances the telephone survey will do as well at a similar cost with a better response rate and less lapse in time. There are studies in which researchers will feel that a personal interviewer is critical, particularly because of the topic, the kinds of measures, or concerns about nonresponse. However, it now is fair to say that instead of having to justify the telephone as the method of choice, researchers are almost in a position of having to justify why they cannot use the telephone.

Finally, it should be clear that the total survey design approach is critical when making a decision regarding mode of data collection. A smaller sample of personal interviews may produce a more useful data set than a larger sample of telephone interviews for the same price. A good sense of methodological goals and thoughtful consideration of all the design issues affecting cost and data quality are necessary before an appropriate decision can be made about how to collect survey data.

EXERCISE

Disregarding monetary costs, describe a survey research problem for which a mail survey would probably be the best choice, and explain why it would be better than the alternatives. Do the same for a random-digit dialed telephone survey; do the same for a personal interview, household survey.

5

Designing Questions to Be Good Measures

In surveys, answers are of interest not intrinsically but because of their relationship to something they are supposed to measure. Good questions are reliable, providing consistent measures in comparable situations, and valid; answers correspond to what they are intended to measure. This chapter discusses theory and practical approaches to designing questions to be reliable and valid measures.

It is always important to remember that designing a question for a survey instrument is designing a measure, not a conversational inquiry. In general, an answer given to a survey question is of no intrinsic interest. Rather the answer is valuable to the extent that it can be shown to have a predictable relationship to facts or subjective states that are of interest. Good questionnaires maximize the relationship between the answers recorded and what the researcher is trying to measure.

In one sense, survey answers are simply responses evoked in an artifical situation contrived by the researcher. What does an answer tell us about some reality in which we have a interest? This question is for the researcher to find out, perhaps to prove.

Let us look at a few specific kinds of answers and their meanings:

(1) A respondent tells us that he voted for Nixon rather than McGovern for president in 1972. The reality in which we are interested is which lever, if any, he pulled in the voting booth. The answer given in the survey may differ from what happened in the voting booth for any number of reasons. The respondent may have pulled the wrong lever and, therefore, not know for whom he voted. The respondent could have forgotten for whom he voted. The respondent could have altered his answer for some reason on purpose. The interviewer accidently could have checked the wrong box even after an "accurate" answer was given.

(2) A respondent tells us how many times he went to the doctor for medical care during the past year. Is that the same number that the researcher would have come up with had he followed the respondent around for 24 hours a day for 365 days during the past year? Problems of recall, problems of definition of what constitutes a visit to a doctor, and problems of willingness to report accurately may affect the corre-

spondence between the number the respondent gives and the count the researcher would have arrived at independently.

(3) When a respondent rates her public school system as "good," rather than "fair" or "poor," the researcher will want to interpret that answer as reflecting evaluations and perceptions of that school system. If the respondent rated only one school (rather than the whole school system), or tilted the answer to please the interviewer, or understood the question differently from others, her answer may not reflect the feelings the researcher tried to measure.

Although many surveys are analyzed and interpreted as if the reseracher "knows" what the answer means, that, in fact, is very risky. Studies designed to evaluate the correspondence between respondents' answers and "true values" show that many respondents answer many questions very well. However, there also is a considerable amount of lack of correspondence. To *assume* perfect correspondence between the answers people give and some other reality is naive. When it is true, it is usually the result of careful design. In the following sections, we discuss many specific ways researchers can improve the correspondence between respondents' answers and the "true" state of affairs.

One goal of a good measure is to increase question reliability. When two respondents are in the same situation, they should answer the question in the same way. To the extent that there is inconsistency across respondents, random error is introduced and the measurement is less precise. The first part of this chapter deals with how to increase the reliability of questions.

There is also the issue of what a given answer "means" in relation to what a researcher is trying to measure: How well does the answer correspond? The later two sections of this chapter are devoted to validity—the correspondence between answers and "true values"—and ways to improve that correspondence (compare Cronbach & Meehl, 1955).

DESIGNING A RELIABLE INSTRUMENT

One step toward ensuring consistent measurement is that each respondent in a sample is asked the same set of questions. Answers to these questions are recorded. The researcher would like to be able to make the assumption that differences in answers stem from differences among respondents rather than from differences in the stimuli to which respondents are exposed. The question's wording is obviously a central part of the stimulus.

A survey data collection is an interaction between a researcher and a respondent. In a self-administered survey, the researcher speaks directly to the respondent through a written questionnaire. In other surveys, an interviewer reads the researcher's words to the respondent. In either case, the questionnaire is the protocol for one side of the interaction. In order to provide a consistent data collection experience for all respondents, a good questionnaire has the following properties:

(1) The researcher's side of the question and answer process is fully scripted, so that the questions as written fully prepare a respondent to answer questions.
(2) The question means the same thing to every respondent.
(3) The kinds of answers that constitute an appropriate response to the question are communicated consistently to all respondents.

Inadequate Wording

The simplest example of inadequate question wording is when, somehow, the researcher's words do not constitute a complete question.

INCOMPLETE WORDING

Bad	Better
5.1 Age?	What was your age on your last birthday?
5.2 Reason last saw doctor?	What was the medical problem or reason for which you most recently went to a doctor?

Interviewers (or respondents) will have to add words or change words in order to make an answerable question. If the goal is to have respondents all answering the same questions, then it is best if the researcher writes the questions fully.

Sometimes optional wording is required to fit differing respondent circumstances. However, that does not mean that the researcher has to give up writing the questions. A common convention is to put optional wording in parentheses. These words will be used by the interviewer when they are appropriate to the situation and omitted when they are not needed.

EXAMPLES OF OPTIONAL WORDING

5.3 Were you (or anyone living here with you) attacked or beaten up
     by a stranger during the past year?

5.4 Did (he/she) report the attack to the police?

5.5 How old was (EACH PERSON) on (his/her) last birthday?

In 5.3, the parenthetical phrase would be omitted if the interviewer
already knew that the respondent lived alone. However, if more than
one person lived in the household, the interviewer would include it.

The parenthetical choice offered in 5.4 may seem minor. However, the parentheses alerts the interviewer to the fact that a choice
must be made; the proper pronoun is used, and the principle is
maintained that the interviewer need read only the questions exactly
as written in order to present a satisfactory stimulus.

A variation that accomplishes the same thing is illustrated in 5.5.
A format such as that might be used if the same question were to be
asked for each person in a household. Rather than repeat the identical
words endlessly, a single question is written instructing the interviewer to substitute an appropriate designation (your husband/your
son/your oldest daughter).

The above examples permit the interviewer to ask questions that
makes sense and take advantage of knowledge previously gained in
the interview to tailor the questions to the respondent's individual
circumstances. There is another kind of optional wording that is seen
occasionally in questionnaire that is not acceptable.

EXAMPLE OF UNACCEPTABLE OPTIONAL WORDING

5.6 What do you like best about this neighborhood? (We're in-
     terested in anything like houses, the people, the parks, or what-
     ever.)

Presumably, the parenthetical probe was thought to be helpful to
respondents who were havng difficulty in answering the question.
However, from a measurement point of view, it undermines the principle of standardized interviewing. If interviewers use the parenthetical probe when a respondent does not readily come up with an
answer, that subset of respondents will have answered a different
question. Such optional probes usually are introduced when the researcher does not think the initial question is a very good one. The

proper approach is to write a good question in the first place. Interviewers should never be given any options about what questions to
read or how to read them except, as in the examples above, to make
the questions fit the circumstances of a particular respondent in a
standardized way.

The following is a different example of incomplete question wording. There are three errors embedded in the example.

POOR EXAMPLE OF STANDARDIZED WORDING

5.7 I would like you to rate different features of your neighborhood
     as *very good, good, fair,* or *poor.* Please think carefully about
     each item as I read it.
     (a) Public schools
     (b) Parks
     (c) Other

The first problem with 5.7 is the *order* of the main stem. The
response alternatives are read prior to an instruction to think carefully
about the questions. The respondent probably will forget the question.
The interviewer likely will have to do some explaining or rewording.
Second, the words the interviewer needs to ask about the second item on
the list, "parks," are not provided in 5.7. A much better question would
be the following:

BETTER EXAMPLE

5.7a I am going to ask you to rate different features of your neighbor-
      hood. I want you to think carefully about your answers. How
      would you rate (FEATURE)—would you say *very good, good,
      fair,* or *poor*?

This gives the interviewer the wording needed for asking the first
and all subsequent items on the list.

The third problem with the example is the alternative "other."
What is the interviewer to say? It is not uncommon to see "other" on
a list of questions in a form similar to the example. Although occasionally there may be a worthwhile question objective involved, most
often the questionnaire will benefit from dropping the item.

The above examples illustrate questions that could not be
presented consistently to all respondents due to incomplete wording.
Another step needed to increase consistency is to create a set of
questions that flows smoothly and easily. It can be shown that if

questions have awkward or confusing wording, if there are words that are difficult to pronounce, or combinations of words that sound awkward together, interviewers will change the words to make the questions sound better or to make them easier to read. It may be possible to train and supervise interviewers to keep such changes to a minimum. However, good design of the questionnaire will raise the odds of a standardized interview.

Ensuring Consistent Meaning to all Respondents

If all respondents are asked exactly the same questions, one step has been taken to ensure that differences in answers can be attributed to differences in respondents. However, there is a further consideration: The questions should all mean the same thing to all respondents. If two respondents understand the question to mean different things, their answers may be different for that reason alone.

One potential problem is using words that are not understood universally. In general samples, it is important to remember that a range of educational experiences and cultural backgrounds will be represented. Even with well-educated samples, using simple words that are short and widely understood is a sound approach to questionnaire design.

Undoubtedly, a much more common error than using unfamiliar words is the use of terms or concepts that can have multiple meanings. It is impossible to give an exhaustive list of ambiguous terms used in surveys, but the prevalence of misunderstanding of common terms has been well documented by those who have studied the problem (e.g., Belson, 1981).

POORLY DEFINED TERMS

5.8 How many times in the past year have you seen or talked with a
      doctor about your health?

Problem. There are two ambiguous terms or concepts in this question. First, there is basis for uncertainty about what constitutes a doctor. Are only people practicing medicine with M.D. degrees included? If so, then psychiatrists are included, but psychologists, chiropractors, osteopaths, and podiatrists are not included. What about physicians' assistants or nurses who work directly for doctors in doctors' offices? If a person goes to a doctor's office for an inoculation that is given by a nurse, does it count?

Second, what constitutes seeing or talking with a doctor? Do telephone consultations count? Do visits to a doctor's office when the doctor is not seen count?

Solutions. Often the best approach is to provide respondents and interviewers with the definitions they need.

5.8a We are going to ask about visits to doctors and getting medical advice from doctors. In this case, we are interested in all professional personnel who have M.D. degrees or work directly for an M.D. in the office such as a nurse or medical assistant.

When the definition of what is wanted is extremely complicated and would take a very long time to define, as may be the case in this question, an additional constructive approach may be to ask supplementary questions about desired events that particularly are likely to be omitted. For example, visits to psychiatrists, visits for inoculations, and telephone consultations often are underreported and may warrant specific follow-up questions.

POORLY DEFINED TERMS

5.9 Did you eat breakfast yesterday?

Problem. The difficulty is that the definition of breakfast varies widely. Some people consider coffee and a donut anytime before noon to be "breakfast." Others do not consider that they have had breakfast unless it includes a major entree, such as bacon and eggs, and is consumed before 8:00 A.M.

Solutions. There are two approaches to the solution. On the one hand, one might choose to define breakfast:

5.9a For our purposes, let us consider breakfast to be a meal eaten before 10:00 in the morning, which includes some protein such as eggs, meat, or milk, some grain such as toast or cereal, and some fruit or vegetable. Using that definition, did you have breakfast yesterday?

While that often is a very good approach, in this case it is very complicated. Instead of trying to communicate a common definition to respondents, the researcher may simply ask people to report what they consumed before 10:00 A.M. At the coding stage, the "quality" of what was eaten can be evaluated consistently without requiring each respondent to share the same definition.

POORLY DEFINED TERMS

5.10 Do you favor or oppose gun control legislation?

Problem. Gun control legislation can mean banning the legal sale of certain kinds of guns, asking people to register their guns, limiting the number or the kinds of guns that people may possess, or which people may possess them. Answers cannot be interpreted without assumptions about what respondents think the question means. Respondents will undoubtedly interpret the question differently.

> 5.10a One proposal for the control of guns is that no person who ever had been convicted of a violent crime would be allowed to purchase or own a pistol, rifle, or shotgun. Would you oppose or support legislation like that?

One could argue that that is only one of a variety of proposals for gun control. That is exactly the point. If one wants to ask multiple questions about different possible responses to a gun control problem, one should ask separate specific questions that can be understood commonly by all respondents and interpreted by researchers. One does not solve the problem of a complex issue by leaving it to the respondents to decide what questions they want to answer.

The worst way to handle a complex definitional problem is to give interviewers instructions about how to define terms if they are asked. Only respondents who ask will receive the definition; interviewers will not give consistently worded definitions if they are not written in the questionnaire. Thus the researcher will never know what question any particular respondent answered. If a complex term that may require definition must be used, interviewers should be required to read a common definition to all respondents.

The "Don't Know" Option

When respondents are being asked questions about their own lives, feelings, or experiences, a "don't know" response is often a statement that they are unwilling to do the work required to give an answer. On the other hand, sometimes we ask respondents questions about things about which they legitimately do not know. As the object of the questions gets further from their immediate lives, the more plausible and reasonable it is that some respondents will not have adequate knowledge on which to base an answer or will not have formed an opinion or feeling.

There are two approaches to dealing with such a possibility. One simply can ask the questions of all respondents, relying on the respondent to volunteer a "don't know." The alternative is to ask respondents whether or not they feel familiar enough with a topic to have an opinion or feeling about it.

When a researcher is dealing with a topic about which familiarity is high, whether or not a screening question for knowledge is asked is probably not important. However, when there is reason to think that a notable number of respondents will not be familiar with whatever the question is dealing with, it probably is best to ask a screening question about familiarity with the topic. People differ in their willingness to volunteer a "don't know." A screening question for familiarity helps to produce a kind of standardization; most people answering the question then will have at least some minimal familiarity with what they are responding to (Schuman & Presser, 1981).

Specialized Wording for Special Subgroups

Researchers have wrestled with the fact that the vocabularies in different subgroups of the population are not the same. One could argue that standardized measurement actually would require different questions for different subgroups.

Designing different forms of questionnaires for different subgroups almost is never done. Rather methodologists tend to work very hard to attempt to find wording for questions that has consistent meaning across an entire population. Even though there are situations where a question wording is more typical of the speech of one segment of a community than another (most often the better-educated segment), finding exactly comparable words for some other group of the population and then giving interviewers reliable rules for deciding when to ask which version is so difficult that it is likely to produce more unreliability than it reduces.

Standardized Expectations for Type of Response

Thus far we have said it is important to give interviewers a good script so that they can read the questions exactly as worded, and it is important to design questions that mean the same thing to all respondents. The other component of a good question that sometimes is overlooked is that respondents should have the same perception of what constitutes an adequate answer for the question.

The simplest way to give respondents the same perceptions of what constitutes an adequate answer is to provide them with a list of acceptable answers. Such questions are called closed questions. The respondent has to choose one, or sometimes more than one, of a set of alternatives provided by the researcher.

Closed questions are not suitable in all instances. The range of possible answers may be more extensive than it is reasonable to provide. The researcher may not feel that all reasonable answers can be anticipated. For such reasons, the researcher may prefer not to provide a list of alternatives to the respondent. However, that does not free the researcher from structuring the focus of the question and the kind of response wanted as carefully as possible.

5.11 Why did you vote for Candidate A?

Problems. Almost all "why" questions have problems. The reason is that one's sense of causality or frame of references can influence what one talks about. In the particular instance above, the respondent may choose to talk about the strengths of Candidate A, the weaknessess of Candidate B, or the reasons the respondent uses certain criteria ("My mother was a lifelong Democrat"). Hence respondents who see things exactly the same way may answer differently.

Solution. Specify the focus of the answer:

5.11a What characteristics of Candidate A led you to vote for (him/her) over Candidate B?

Such a question explains to respondents that we want them to talk about Candidate A, the person for whom they voted. If all respondents answer with that same frame of reference, we then will be able to compare responses from different respondents in a direct fashion.[1]

5.12 What are some of the things about this neighborhood that you like best?

Problems. In response to a question like that, some people will only make one or two points, while others will make many. It is possible that such differences reflect important differences in respondent perceptions or feelings. However, research has shown pretty clearly that education is related highly to the number of answers people give to questions. Interviewers also affect the number of such answers.

Solution. Specify the number of points to be made:

5.12a What is the feature of this neighborhood that you would single out as the one you like most?

5.12b Tell me the three things about this neighborhood that you like most about living here.

Although that may not be a satisfactory solution for all questions, for many such questions it is an effective way of reducing unwanted variation in answers across respondents.

The basic point is that answers can vary because respondents have a different understanding of the kind of responses that are appropriate. Better specification of the properties of the answer desired can remove a needless source of unreliability in the measurement process.

TYPES OF MEASURES/TYPES OF QUESTIONS

Introduction

The above procedures are designed to maximize reliability—the extent to which people in comparable situations will answer questions in similar ways. However, one can measure with perfect reliability and still not be measuring what one wants to measure. The extent to which the answer given is a true measure and means what the researcher wants it to mean or expects it to mean is called validity. In this section, we discuss other aspects of the design of questionnaires, in addition to steps to maximize the reliability of questions, that can increase the validity of survey measures.

For this discussion, it is necessary to differentiate questions designed to measure facts or objectively measurable events from questions designed to measure subjective states such as attitudes, opinions, and feelings. Even though there are questions that fall in a murky area on the borders of these two categories, the idea of validity is somewhat different for subjective and objective measures for several reasons.

If it is possible to check the accuracy of an answer by some independent observation, then the measure of validity becomes the similarity of the survey report to the value of some "true" measure. In theory, one could obtain an independent, accurate count of the number of times that an individual obtained medical services from a physician during a year. Although in practice it may be very difficult to obtain such an independent measure (e.g., records also contain errors), the understanding of validity can be consistent for objective situations.

In contrast, when people are asked about subjective states, feelings, attitudes, and opinions, there is no objective way of validating the answers. Only the person has access to his or her feelings and opinions. Thus the only way of assessing the "validity" of reports of subjective states is the way in which they correlate either with other answers that a person gives or with other facts about the person's life that one thinks should be related to what is being measured. For such measures, there is no truly independent direct measure possible; the meaning of answers must be inferred from patterns of association. This fundamental difference in the meaning of validity requires separate discussions regarding ways of maximizing validity.

Levels of Measurement

There are four different ways in which measurement is carried out in social sciences. This produces four different kinds of tasks for respondents and four different kinds of data for analysis:

(1) *Nominal*—people or events are sorted into unordered categories. ("Are you male or female?")
(2) *Ordinal*—people or events are ordered or placed in ordered categories along a single dimension. ("How would you rate your health—very good, good, fair, or poor?")
(3) *Interval data*—numbers are attached that provide meaningful information about the distance between ordered stimuli or classes. (In fact, interval data are very rare; Fahrenheit temperature readings are among the few common examples.)
(4) *Ratio data*—numbers are assigned that have absolute meaning such as a count or measurement by an objective, physical scale such as distance, weight, or pressure. ("How old were you on your last birthday?")

Most often in surveys, when one is collecting factual data, respondents are asked to fit themselves or their experiences into a category, creating nominal data, or they are asked for a number, most often ratio data. "Are you employed?", "Are you married?", and "Do you have arthritis?" are examples of questions that provide nominal data. "How many times have you seen a doctor?", "How old are you?", and "What is your income?" are examples of questions to which respondents are asked to provide real numbers for ratio data.

When gathering factual data, respondents may be asked for ordinal answers. For example, they may be asked to report their incomes in relatively large categories or to describe their behavior in nonnumerical terms ("usually, occasionally, seldom, or never"). When respondents are asked to report factual events in ordinal terms, it is because great precision is not required by the researcher or because the task of reporting an exact number was considered too difficult; ordinal classification seemed a more realistic task for a respondent. However, there usually is a real numerical basis underlying an ordinal answer to a factual question.[2]

The situation is somewhat different with respect to reports of subjective data. Although there have been efforts over the years, first in the work of a psychophysical psychologists (e.g., Thurstone, 1929), to have people assign numbers to subjective states that met the assumptions of interval and ratio data, for the most part respondents are asked to provide nominal and ordinal data about subjective states. The nominal question is, "Into which category do your feelings, opinions, or perceptions fall?" The ordinal question is, "Where along this continuum do your feelings, opinions, or perceptions fall?"

When designing a questionnaire, a basic task of the researcher is to decide what kind of measurement is desired. When that decision is made, there are some clear implications for the form in which the question will be asked.

Types of Questions

Survey questions can be classified roughly into two groups: those for which a list of acceptable responses is provided to the respondent (closed questions) and those for which the acceptable responses are not provided exactly to the respondent (open questions).

When the goal is to put people in unordered categories (nominal data), the researcher has a choice about whether to ask an open or closed question. Virtually identical questions can be designed in either form.

EXAMPLES OF OPEN AND CLOSED FORMS

5.13   What health conditions do you have? (Open)

5.13a Which of the following conditions do you currently have? (READ LIST.) (Closed)

5.14   What do you consider to be the most important problem facing our country today? (Open)

5.14a Here is a list of problems that many people in the country are concerned about. Which do you consider to be the most important problem facing our country today? (Closed)

There are advantages to open questions. They permit the researcher to obtain answers that were unanticipated. They also may describe more closely the real views of the respondent. Third, and this is not a trivial point, respondents like the opportunity to answer some questions in their own words. To answer only by choosing a provided response and never to have an opportunity to say what is on one's mind can be a frustrating experience. Finally, open questions are appropriate when the list of possible answers is longer than it is feasible to present to respondents.

Having said all this, closed questions are usually a more satisfactory way of creating data. There are three reasons for this:

(1) The respondent can perform more reliably the task of answering the question when response alternatives are given.

(2) The researcher can perform more reliably the task of interpreting the meaning of answers when the alternatives are given to the respondent (Schuman & Presser, 1981).

(3) When a completely open question is asked, many people give relatively rare answers that are not analytically useful. Providing respondents with a constrained number of categories increases the likelihood that there will be enough people in any given category to be analytically interesting.

Finally, if the researcher wants ordinal data, the categories must be provided to the respondent. One cannot order responses reliably along a single continuum unless a set of permissable ordered answers is specified in the question. A bit more about the task that is given to respondents when they are asked to perform an ordinal task is appropriate, since it is probably the most prevalent kind of measurement in survey research.

Figure 5.1 shows a continuum. In this case we are talking about having respondents make a rating of some sort, but the general approach applies to all ordinal questions. There is a dimension that is assumed by the researcher that goes from the most negative feelings possible to the most positive feelings possible. The way survey researchers get respondents into ordered categories is to put designations or labels on such a continuum. Respondents then are asked to consider the labels, consider their own feelings or opinions, and place themselves in the proper category.

There are two points worth making about the kinds of data that result from such questions. First, respondents will differ one from the other in their understanding of what the labels or categories mean. However, the only assumption that is necessary in order to make meaningful analyses is that, on the average, the people who rate their feelings as "good" feel more positively than those who rate their feelings "fair." To the extent that people differ some in their understanding of and criteria for "good" and "fair," there is unreliability in the measurement, but the measurement still may have meaning (i.e., correlate with the underlying feeling state that the researcher wants to measure).

Second, an ordinal scale measurement like this is relative. *The distribution of people choosing a particular label or category depends on the particular scale that is presented.*

Consider the rating scale in Figure 5.1 again and consider two approaches to creating ordinal scales. In one case, the researcher used a three-point scale, "good, fair, or poor." In the second case, the researcher used five descriptive words, "excellent, very good, good, fair, and poor." When one compares the two scales, one can see that adding "excellent" and "very good" in all probability does not simply break up the "good" catergory into three pieces. Rather it changes the whole sense of the scale. People respond to the ordinal position of categories as well as to the descriptors. "Fair" almost certainly is further to the negative side of the continuum when it is the fourth point on the scale than when it is the second. Thus one would expect considerably more people to give a rating of "good" or better with the five-point scale than with the three-point scale.

Such scales are meaningful if used as they are supposed to be used: to order people. However, by itself a statement that some percentage of the population feels something is "good or better" is not appropriate because it implies that the population is being described in some absolute sense. The percentage would change if the question were different. Only comparative statements (or statements about relationships) are justifiable when one is using ordinal measures:

(a) Comparing answers to the same question across groups; e.g., 20 percent more of those in Group A than in Group B rated the candidate as "good" or better; or

(b) Comparing answers from comparable samples over time, e.g., 10 percent more rate the candidate "good" or better in January than did so in November.

The same general comments apply to data obtained by having respondents order items. ("Consider the schools, police services, and

trash collection. Which is the most important city service to you?")
The percentage giving any item top ranking, or the average ranking of
an item, is completely dependent on the particular list provided.
Comparisons between distributions when the alternatives have been
changed at all are not meaningful.

Agree-Disagree Items: A Special Case

Agree-disagree items are very prevalent in the survey research
field and therefore deserve special attention. One can see that the task
that respondents are given in such items is different from that of
placing themselves in an ordered category. The usual approach is to
read a statement to respondents and ask them if they agree or disagree
with that statement. The statement is located somewhere on a continuum such as that portrayed in Figure 5.1. Respondents' locations on
that continuum are calculated by figuring out whether they say they are
very close to that statement (by agreeing) or saying their feelings are very
far from where that statement is located (by disagreeing).

The use of agree-disagree questions to order respondents has two
main potential limits.

First, a statement, in order to be interpretable, must be located at
the end of a continuum. For example, if a statement was to be rated
that said "The schools are fair," presumably a point in the middle of a
continuum, a respondent could disagree either because he rated the
schools as "good" or because he rated them as "poor." The similiar
limitation is that it is very common for the statements used as stimuli
for agree-disagree questions to have more than one dimension, (i.e.,
to be double-barrelled), in which case the answer cannot be interpreted. The two statements below provide examples of double-
barrelled statements.

5.15 In the next five years, this country will probably be strong and
prosperous.

Problems. It obviously is possible for someone to have the view
that the country will be strong but not prosperous or vice-versa. Since
prosperity and strength do not go together necessarily, a respondent
may have trouble knowing what to do.

5.16 With economic conditions the way they are these days, it really
isn't fair to have more than one or two children.

Problems. If a person does not happen to think that economic
conditions are terrible (which the question imposes as an assump-

FEELING ABOUT SOMETHING

| EXTREMELY | | EXTREMELY |
| POSITIVE | | NEGATIVE |

TWO-CATEGORY SCALE

| GOOD | NOT GOOD |

THREE-CATEGORY SCALE

| GOOD | FAIR | POOR |

FOUR-CATEGORY SCALE

| VERY GOOD | GOOD | FAIR | POOR |

FIVE-CATEGORY SCALE

| EXCELLENT | VERY GOOD | GOOD | FAIR | POOR |

Figure 5.1 Subjective Continuum Scale

tion,) and/or if a person does not believe that economic conditions of whatever kind have any implications for family size, but if that person happens to think one or two children is a good target for a family, it is not easy to answer the question. The problem then is knowing what the respondent agreed to, if he or she agreed. Asking two or three questions at once and having imbedded assumptions in questions are very common problems with the agree-disagree format. The agree-disagree format appears to be a rather simple way to construct questionnaires. In fact, to use this form to provide reliable, useful measures is not easy and requires a great deal of care and attention. In many cases, researchers would have more reliable and interpretable measures if they used a different question form.

INCREASING THE VALIDITY OF
FACTUAL REPORTING

When a researcher asks a factual question of a respondent, the goal is to have the respondent report with perfect accuracy; that is, give the same answer that the researcher would have given if the researcher had access to the information needed to answer the question. There is a rich methodological literature on the reporting of factual material. Reporting has been compared against records in a variety of areas, in particular the reporting of economic and health events (see Cannell et al., 1977a, for a good summary).

Respondents answer many questions accurately. For example, over 90 percent of overnight hospital stays within six months of an interview are reported (Cannell & Fowler, 1965). However, how well people report depends on both what they are being asked and how the question is asked.

There are four basic reasons why respondents report events with less than perfect accuracy:

(1) They do not know the information.
(2) They cannot recall it, although they do know it.
(3) They do not understand the question.
(4) They do not want to report the answer in the interview context.

There are several steps that the researcher can take to combat each of these potential problems. Let us review these.

Lack of Knowledge

Since the main point of doing a survey is to get information from repondents that is not available in other ways, most surveys deal with questions to which repondents know the answers. The main reason that a researcher would get inaccurate reporting due to lack of knowledge is that he or she is asking one household member for information that another household member has. In health surveys, for example, it is common to use a household informant to report on visits to the doctor, hospitalizations, and illnesses for all household members. Economic and housing surveys often ask for a household respondent to report information for the household as a whole.

If the information exists in the household, but simply not with the person that the researcher wants to be the main respondent, the solutions are either to eliminate proxy reporting or to provide an opportunity for respondents to consult with other family members. For example, the National Crime Survey conducted by the Census Bureau obtains reports of household crimes from a single household informant, but in addition asks each household adult directly about personal crimes such as robbery. If the basic interview is to be carried out in person, costs for interviews with other members of the household can be reduced if self-administered forms are left to be filled out by absent household members, or if secondary interviews are done by telephone. A variation is to ask the main respondent to report the desired information as fully as possible for all household members. Then mail the respondent a summary for verification, permitting consultation with other family members (see Cannell & Fowler, 1965).

Finally, it sometimes is worth asking household members to designate the best informed person to answer the questions. The housewife is not always the most knowledgeable about health, and the husband is not always the most knowledgeable about finances. People themselves often can do a better job of choosing the best respondent for a particular topic than can the researcher.

Recall

Studies of the reporting of known hospital stays clearly show the significance of memory in the reporting of events. As the time between the interview and a hospitalization event increases, the probability of it being reported in an interview decreases. In a like way, short hospitalizations are less likely to be reported than long ones. Memory decays in predictable ways; the minor and distant events are more difficult to conjure up in a quick question and answer interview.

There are several ways to reduce the impact of memory decay on the reporting of factual events. Five possible methods are as follows:

(1) Reduce the period of time about which respondents are asked to report. There is great value in having respondents report for as long

a period of time as possible, because there is more information obtained in that way. However, the longer the reporting period, the less accurate the reporting (Cannell & Fowler, 1965).

(2) Memory is improved by asking more questions. By asking more than one question about events, more time will elapse for the respondent to think. In addition, questions can be designed that will stimulate associations, thereby helping the recall process. Thus the number of health conditions reported is increased by asking about visits to doctors, taking medications, and missing work (Madow, 1963).

(3) A second chance to think about the answers given also can stimulate memory. The technique suggested above of sending the respondent a summary of answers for verification has been shown to improve the recall process as well; even asking for the same information twice in the same interview can help recall.

(4) A reinterview procedure, interviewing the same respondent twice or even more times, is another good way to deal with problems of recall. One key problem with recalling events over time is getting them in the proper time period. An initial interview can serve as an anchorpoint for people's recall. The previous interview serves as a boundary in their minds. In addition, the researcher can check to make sure that events reported in Interview 1 were not repeated in Interview 2. A final advantage of the panel approach is that respondents are sensitized to the kinds of events that will be asked about, thereby further improving their recall.

(5) Carrying that last point a step further, one way that researchers have dealt with the reporting of minor events that are hard to remember is by asking people to keep a diary. Consumption patterns, minor deviations from good health, and patterns of expenditure are all difficult for people to recall in detail over time unless they are taking notes. Even respondents who do not keep their diaries up to date conscientiously report considerably better than they would have had they not been keeping a diary (Sudman & Bradburn, 1974).

It should be noted that a trade-off with both the reinterview and diary strategies is that it is more difficult to convince people to keep a diary or be interviewed several times than it is to get them to agree to a one-time interview. Hence the values of improved reporting have to be weighed against the possible biases resulting from sample attrition.

Social Desirability

There are certain facts or events that respondents rather would not report accurately in an interview. Conditions that have some degree of social undesirability such as mental illness and venereal disease are underreported significantly more than other conditions

(Madow, 1963; Densen et al., 1963). Hospitalization associated with conditions that are particularly threatening, either because of the possible stigmas that may be attached to them or due to their life threatening nature, are reported at a lower rate than average (Cannell et al., 1977a). Aggregate estimates of alcohol consumption strongly suggest underreporting, although the reporting problems may be a combination of recall difficulties and respondents' concerns about social norms regarding drinking. Arrest and bankruptcy are other events that have been found to be underreported consistently, but which seem unlikely to have been forgotten (Locander et al., 1976).

There are probably limits to what people will report in a standard interview setting. If a researcher realistically expects someone to admit something that is very embarrassing or illegal, extraordinary efforts are needed to convince respondents that the risks are minimal and the reasons for taking a risk are substantial. The following are some of the steps that a researcher might particularly consider when sensitive questions are being asked (also see Sudman & Bradburn, 1982).

(1) *Minimize a sense of judgment;* maximize the importance of accuracy. Careful attention to the introduction and vocabulary that might imply that the researcher would value negatively certain answers is important.

Researchers always have to be aware of the fact that respondents are having a conversation with the researcher. The questionnaire, plus the behavior of the interviewer if there is one, constitutes all the information the respondent has about the kind of interpretation the researcher will give to the answers. Therefore, the researcher needs to be very careful about the kind of cues the respondent is receiving and about the type of context in which respondents feel their answers will be interpreted.

(2) *Use self-administered questions.* Although the data are not conclusive, there is evidence that telephone interviews are more subject to social-desirability bias than personal interviews (e.g., Henson et al., 1977; Mangione et al., 1982); there is also evidence that having respondents answer questions in a self-administered form rather than having an interviewer ask the questions may produce less social-desirability bias for some items (e.g., Hochstim, 1967). Such a consideration might lead one to think of a mail survey or group administration. A personal interview survey also can be combined usefully with self-administration: A respondent simply is given a set of questions to answer in a booklet as part of the personal interview experience.

(3) *Confidentiality and anonymity.* Almost all surveys promise respondents that answers will be treated confidentially and that no one outside the research staff will ever be able to associate individual

respondents with their answers. Respondents usually are reassured of such facts by interviewers in the introduction and in advance letters, if there are any; these may be reinforced by signed commitments from the researchers. For surveys on particularly sensitive or personal subjects, special steps to ensure that respondents cannot be linked to their answers (such as the random response techniques described by Greenberg et al., 1969) may be used.

Again it is important to emphasize that the limit of survey research is what people are willing to tell researchers under the conditions of data collection designed by the researcher. There are some questions that probably cannot be asked of probability samples without extraordinary efforts (e.g., Kinsey et al., 1948). However, some of the procedures discussed in this section, such as trying to create a neutral context for answers and emphasizing the importance of accuracy and the neutrality of the data collection process, are probably worthwhile procedures for the most innocuous of questions. Any question, no matter how innocent it may seem, may embarrass somebody in the sample. It is best to design all phases of a survey instrument with a sensitivity to reducing the effects of social desirability and embarrassment on any answers people may give.

INCREASING VALIDITY OF SUBJECTIVE QUESTIONS

As discussed above, the validity of subjective questions has a different meaning than the validity of objective questions. There is no external criterion. One only can estimate the validity of a subjective measure by the extent to which answers are associated in expected ways with the answers to other questions or other characteristics of the individual to which it should be related (see Turner & Martin, 1984, for an extensive discussion of issues affecting the validity of subjective measures).

There basically are only three steps to the improvement of validity of subjective measures:

(1) Make the questions as reliable as possible. Review the sections on the reliability of questions, dealing with ambiguity of wording, standardized presentation, and vagueness in response form, and do everything possible to get questions that will mean the same thing to all respondents. To the extent that subjective measures are unreliable, their validity will be reduced.

A special issue is the reliability of ordinal scales, which are dominant as measure of subjective states. The response alternatives offered must be unidimensional (deal with only one issue) and monotonic (presented in order, without inversion).

PROBLEMATIC SCALES

5.16 How would you rate your job—very rewarding, rewarding but stressful, not very rewarding but not stressful, or not rewarding at all?

5.17 How would you rate your job—very rewarding, somewhat rewarding, rewarding, or not rewarding at all?

Question 5.16 has two scaled properties—rewardingness and stress—that need not be related. All the alternatives are not played out. Question 5.16 should be made into two questions if rewardingness and stress of jobs are both to be measured. In 5.17, some would see "rewarding" as more positive than "somewhat rewarding" and be confused about how the categories were ordered. Both of these problems are common and should be avoided.

(2) When putting people into ordered classes along a continuum, it probably is better to have more categories than fewer. There is a limit, however, in the precision of discrimination that respondents can exercise in giving ordered ratings. When the number of categories exceeds the respondents' ability to discriminate their feelings, numerous categories simply produce unreliable "noise." However, the validity of a measure will be increased to the extent that real variation among repondents is measured.

(3) Ask multiple questions, with different question forms, that measure the same subjective state; combine the answers into a scale. The answers to all questions potentially are influenced both by the subjective state to be measured and by specific features of the respondent or of the questions. Some respondents avoid extreme categories; some tend to agree more than disagree; others do just the opposite. Multiple questions help even out response idiosyncracies and improve the validity of the measurement process (Cronbach, 1951).

The most important point to remember about the meaning of subjective measures is their relativity. Distributions can be compared only when the stimulus situation is the same; small changes in wording, changing the number of alternatives offered, and even changing the position of a question in a questionnaire can make a major difference in how people answer. (See Turner & Martin, 1984; Schuman & Presser, 1981; and Sudman & Bradburn, 1982 for numerous examples of factors that affect response distributions.) The distribution of answers to a subjective question cannot be interpreted directly; it only has meaning when differences between samples exposed to the same questions are compared or when patterns of association among answers are studied.

ERROR IN PERSPECTIVE

A defining property of social surveys is that answers to questions are used as measures. The extent to which those answers are good measures is obviously a critical dimension of the quality of survey estimates.

Questions can be poor measures because they are unreliable (producing erratic results) or because they are biased, producing estimates that consistently err in one direction from the true value (as when drunk driving arrests are underreported).

We know quite a bit about how to make questions reliable. The principles outlined in this chapter to increase reliability are probably sound. Although other points might be added to the list, creating unambiguous questions that provide consistent measures across respondents is always a constructive step for good measurement.

The validity issue is more complex. In a sense, each variable to be measured requires research to identify the best set of questions to measure it and to produce estimates of how valid the resulting measure is. Many of the suggestions to improve reporting in this chapter emerged from a twenty-year program to evaluate and improve the measurement of health-related variables (Cannell et al., 1977a, 1977b). There are many areas in which a great deal more work on validation is needed.

A third issue is the credibility of a question (or series) as a measure. It always is legitimate to ask researchers for their evidence about how well a question (or series) measures what it is supposed to. Too often, researchers make little effort to evaluate their measures; they assume, and ask their readers to assume, that answers mean what they "look like" they mean and measure what the researcher thinks they are supposed to measure. To rely on so-called "face validity" of questions is not acceptable practice.

Researchers should build explicit efforts to assess the validity of their key meausres into their analyses. As standard practice, patterns of association related to validity can be calculated and presented in an appendix.

Reducing measurement error through better question design is one of the least costly ways to improve survey estimates. For any survey, it is reasonable to attend to careful questionnaire design and pretesting (which are discussed in Chapter 6) and making use of the existing research literature about how to measure what is to be measured. Also, building a literature over time in which the validity of measures has been evaluated and reported is much needed. Such evaluations are now the exception; they should become routine.

EXERCISES

1. Use the criteria discussed in this chapter to evaluate the following questions as reliable, interpretable, and analytically useful measures; write better questions if you can.

(a) To measure *income:* "How much do you make?"

(b) To measure *health:* "How healthy are you?"

(c) To measure *satisfaction with life:* "How would you rate your life— *very good, better than average, mixed, could be better,* or *very bad?"*

(d) To measure *opinions about abortion laws:* "Tell me whether you agree or disagree with the following statement: Abortion is morally very questionable; abortions should be illegal, except in emergencies."

2. Write a hypothesis about a possible relationship between two variables. (Example: Good health is associated with receiving good quality health care; or good quality housing is related to having a high income.) Then under each part of the hypothesis, write the information you would need in order to assign a value to a person for each of the two variables. Then draft a question (or set of questions) for each part, the answers to which would provide the information you need. Indicate whether your questions ask for factual or subjective information and whether the resulting data will have nominal, ordinal, interval, or ratio properties.

NOTES

1. It could be argued that whether it is attraction for A or aversion to B that led to the vote might be of interest. True. However, 5.11 is not a reliable way to find that out. If that truly is an objective, the solution is to ask directly, "Did you mainly vote for A or against B?"

2. A respondent may be given an ordinal task—such as reporting income in categories—and through interpolation the researcher may try to construct interval or ratio estimates.

6

Design of a Questionnaire

Designing a good questionnaire involves selecting the questions needed to meet the research objectives, testing them to make sure they can be asked and answered as planned, then putting them into a form to maximize the ease with which respondents and interviewers can do their jobs. This chapter describes steps for designing good questionnaires.

Understanding what a good question is and how to use questions as measures, as discussed in Chapter 5, is certainly the foundation of good questionnaire design. There is, however, a series of very practical steps needed to produce a good data collection instrument. This chapter presents a summary of those steps. Sudman and Bradburn (1982), Dillman (1978), and De Maio (1983) provide longer, more detailed discussions of such steps.

DEFINING OBJECTIVES

A prerequisite to designing a good questionnaire is deciding what is to be measured. That may seem simple and self-evident, but it is a step that often is overlooked to the detriment of questionnaires.

One valuable first step is to write a paragraph about what the survey is supposed to accomplish. In designing a questionnaire, researchers often are tempted to add related questions that do not contribute to achieving the project's goals. One check against such temptations is to have a good statement of the purposes, against which the inclusion of a particular area of inquiry can be measured.

Second, one should make a list of what should be measured to accomplish the goals of the project. These should not be questions. They should be variables to be measured. They should be listed in categories or areas that make sense.

An analysis plan should be developed to go with the list of variables to be measured. Presumably, a good start already will have been made in connection with the design of the sample. The researcher will have had to think through which subgroups in the population require special estimates. At this point, however, the researcher should refine those ideas, so that there is a clear idea of (1) which variables are designed to be dependent variables, for which measures of central tendency such as means or distributions are to be estimated; (2) which variables are needed as independent variables in order to understand distributions and patterns of association; and (3) which variables may be needed as control or intervening variables to explain patterns observed and to check out competing hypotheses.

These three documents—a statement of purposes, a list of the kinds of variables to be measured, and a draft of an analysis plan—are essential components to developing a questionnaire.

FOCUSED DISCUSSION

Before writing a draft of a structured set of questions, it often is valuable to conduct focused discussions in which the questions are not structured fully. There are many ways this can be accomplished. One approach is to bring together a few groups of five or ten people representative of the study population to discuss the topics to be covered in the survey. A leader keeps the conversation focused on a preset agenda and asks questions to clarify comments.

Such discussions help the researcher to understand the way people talk about the survey issues, which in turn can help in choosing vocabulary and phrasing questions. In addition, such groups frequently suggest issues, concerns, or ways of looking at the topic that the researcher had not thought of.

Efforts to talk with members of the study population before designing a survey instrument can be fruitfully much more elaborate than the approach just described. Less formal efforts also can be valuable. However, virtually any survey effort would benefit from such efforts prior to questionnaire design. The greater the importance of and investment to be made in the survey, the more sensible it is to invest in preliminary, focused discussions prior to designing the questionnaire.

FRAMING QUESTIONS

Armed with a list of what is to be measured, the researcher attempts to find the single question or set of questions needed to create measures of the variables on the list. Many questions, such as those dealing with background or demographic issues, are standard to many surveys. Reviewing the questions in the General Social Survey carried out by the National Opinion Research Center, University of Chicago, may be useful. Copies of original survey instruments from any of the major survey organizations also are useful as references. From these questionnaires, the researcher will glean ideas about how specific questions are phrased, how to generate standardized questions, and how to format questionnaires.

Taking advantage of the work that others have done is very sensible. Of course, it is best to review questions asked by researchers who have done previous work on the study topic. In addition, if questions have been asked of other samples, collecting comparable data may add to the generalizability of the research. However, the mere fact that someone else has used a question before is no guarantee that it is a very good question or, certainly, that it is an appropriate question for a given survey. Many bad questions are asked over and over again, because researchers uncritically use them over and over again.

Ideally, one would like evidence from previous research regarding a question's validity—how well it measures what it is supposed to measure. There are four practical standards that all questions should meet:

(1) Is this a question that can be asked exactly the way it is written?
(2) Is this a question that will mean the same thing to everyone?
(3) Is this a question that people can answer?
(4) Is this a question that people will be willing to answer, given the data collection procedures?

Formal pretesting, which will be discussed below, is an invaluable part of the questionnaire design process. However, at early stages of framing questions, the researcher can learn a great deal by trying out questions on friends, relatives, and co-workers. Early versions of most questionnaires contain questions that are confusing, that cannot be read as written, and that are virtually unanswerable by anyone. Before actually transforming a set of questions into a pretest questionnaire, the researcher will benefit from informal efforts to identify problems in the wording of questions.

DESIGN, FORMAT, AND LAYOUT
OF THE QUESTIONNAIRE

Once a set of questions is close to ready for pretesting, they need to be put into a form to facilitate interviewer or self-administration.

A first step is simply to order the questions. Many researchers like to start with relatively easy, straightforward questions that help "get the respondent into" the survey. Questions requiring a good deal of thought, or those thought to be sensitive, often are reserved for the middle or later sections of questionnaires. The flow of the questionnaire also may dictate some ordering, particularly if interviewers need some answers in order to know if other questions apply.

A good practical step is to number questions in sections: A1, A2, . . ., B1, B2, . . ., etc. In this way, when questions are added or deleted, it is not necessary to renumber every question.

Whether the survey is to be interviewer-administered or self-administered, the goal of the layout and format of the questionnaire should be to make the tasks of the interviewer and the respondent as easy as possible. For an interviewer-administered survey instrument, the following are some rules that will help achieve that goal:

(1) Adopt a convention that differentiates between the words that interviewers are to read to respondents and words that are instructions. A common convention is to use upper case letters for instructions and lower case for questions to be read aloud.

(2) Establish a clear convention for handling instructions to skip questions that do not apply to a particular respondent. The instructions should be keyed to a particular response and tell the interviewer where to go to ask the next question. Some organizations rely heavily on the visual cues of boxes and arrows, which probably are the most self-explanatory. However, such visual cues require a good bit of formatting at the typing and printing stages of the questionnaire. Other organizations simply have clearly written SKIP instructions. Whatever approach is used, it is worthwhile to be completely consistent so that interviewers do not have to spend time thinking about which questions to ask.

(3) Put optional wording in parentheses. Conventions such as (his/her) or (husband/wife) are easy for interviewers to handle smoothly if they are alerted by the parentheses. A similar convention uses all caps (e.g., SPOUSE) when the interviewer must supply a word that is not provided in the question itself.

(4) Check to make sure that all the words that an interviewer has to say are, in fact, written. This includes not only the phrasing of the

questions; it also includes transitions, introductions to questions, needed definitions, and explanations.

For self-administered questionnaires, the same kind of general principles apply; that is, the main goal is to make it easy to use. If anything, the formatting of a self-administered questionnaire is more important. In contrast to interviewers, respondents do not receive the benefit of training, they usually are not motivated to do the job well, and they are not selected on the basis of their ability to handle questionnaires. Six guiding principles are as follows:

(1) A self-administered questionnaire should be self-explanatory. Reading instructions should not be necessary, because they will not be read consistently.

(2) Self-administered questionnaires should be restricted to closed answers. Checking a box or circling a number should be the only task required. When respondents are asked to answer in their own words, the answers usually are incomplete, vague, and difficult to code, and therefore are of only limited value as measurements.

(3) The question forms in a self-administered questionnaire should be few in number. The more the questionnaire can be set up so that the respondent has the same kinds of tasks and questions to answer, the less likely it is that respondents will become confused; also, the easier the task will be for the respondents.

(4) A questionnaire should be typed and laid out in a way that seems clear and uncluttered. Photoreduction, or other strategies for putting many questions on a page, actually reduces the response rate compared with when the same number of questions are spaced attractively over more pages.

(5) Skip patterns should be kept to a minimum. If some respondents must skip some questions, arrows and boxes that communicate skips without verbal instructions are best.

(6) Provide redundant information to respondents. If people can be confused about what they are supposed to do, they will be.

PRETESTING

Every questionnaire should be pretested, no matter how skilled the researcher. Virtually every questionnaire could be changed in some way to make it easier for respondents and interviewers to meet the researcher's objectives. Obviously, the closer the final instrument is to perfection, the better the research process. Once the final questionnaires are printed and data collection has begun, changes are expensive and very difficult to make; already completed interviews have to be eliminated from the analysis if question wording is changed.

Pretesting an Interview Schedule

A minimal pretest would involve having senior, experienced interviewers interview from ten to twenty respondents. Although a representative sample is not needed, the pretest sample should include the range of education and life situations that one would expect to find in the final sample.

It does not hurt to tell respondents that one purpose of their interview is to ensure that questions and procedures work properly. No deceit need be involved in the pretest. However, it is important that the respondents be strangers to the interviewer in order to get a reading on the response to the survey experience as well as to the process of answering questions. In fact the more realistic the pretest, the more the researcher can learn about all aspects of the planned study procedures.

From a minimal pretest, the main information will be from reports of the interviewers about the question and answer process and respondent reactions. Thus interviewers who have worked on other surveys and have a good sense of what a standardized interview is about are needed in order to provide realistic evaluations and useful impressions. Good pretest interviewers will identify questions that were hard to read as written or that were hard for respondents to understand. They also can note mechanical problems, such as interviewer instruction errors, inadequate space for recording, or inappropriate sequencing of questions.

The value of pretests can be strengthened if interviews are tape-recorded and systematically coded. Noting the frequency with which a question requires repeating, probing, or clarification can provide clues to problem questions.

The value of tape recording and coding pretest interviews is considerably enhanced if a larger pretest of, say, 40 or 50 interviews is done. Moreover, small pretests can identify potential problems in wording or questionnaire mechanics but provide little information related to the content of questions and answers. With a larger pilot study, the distributions of answers can be tabulated. Even though a pretest sample is unlikely to be representative of the population as a whole, distributions that are markedly different from what is desired or expected can suggest candidates for revision. In addition, patterns of association can be examined. If there are questions that have not been used before, analysis of correlations can give some indication of whether or not questions are measuring what is expected. Although such an effort does not provide a guarantee against asking poor or invalid questions, it does provide an opportunity to identify some problems with questions that can be alleviated before major field work begins.

Pretesting a Self-Administered Questionnaire

If anything, self-administered questionnaires require more pretesting than interviewer-administered questionnaires, simply because interviewers can solve some problems the researcher did not solve in the design of the questionnaire. A pretest mailing to a sample of potential respondents may produce useful estimates of the rate of return as well as the distribution of responses that can be expected. However, it does not do a great deal for identifying problems with the questionnaire. The value of such a pretest can be enhanced by asking a set of questions specifically about the questionnaire itself: whether there were confusing questions, questions that were difficult to answer, and the like.

Probably the best way to pretest a self-administered questionnaire is in person with a group of potential respondents. First, respondents are asked to complete the questionnaire. Then the investigator leads a discussion about the questionnaire. Respondents are asked to identify confusing and difficult questions. Particular attention is focused on the instructions. Discussion of the meaning of the answers that were given also is useful. Such discussion helps to identify questions that respondents misunderstand or misinterpret as well as format or design problems.

QUESTIONNAIRE LENGTH

One outcome of a good pretest is to find out how long it takes to complete a questionnaire. The criteria for interview length should include cost, effect on response rate, and the limits of respondent ability and willingness to answer questions.

The extent to which the length of a self-administered questionnaire affects costs and response rates varies with the population being studied and the topic. Generalizations are difficult.

It also is difficult to generalize about how long people can be interviewed. The Federal Office of Management and Budget has set as a guideline that surveys should take less than half an hour unless there is compelling reason why more information is needed. However, there are many academic surveys that last an hour or longer.

When researchers find that they have more questions to ask than they feel they can ask, there are two choices available. Of course, the researcher simply may cut questions. An alternative approach is to assign subsets of questions to representative subsamples of respondents. Such an approach increases the complexity of the survey and reduces the precision of estimates of those variables, but may be preferable to leaving out questions altogether.

CONCLUSION

In general, there probably is a lack of appreciation of the importance of the way a questionnaire is designed for reducing the total amount of error in survey estimates. Unfortunately, questionnaire design has been seen in the past as an art rather than a science. The rules enunciated by Stanley Payne (1951), based largely on his own experience, are seen by some to be the limits of our wisdom about how to design questionnaires. Yet over the past twenty years there have been advances in our understanding of the way that questionnaire design can improve the quality of data.

Moreover, although many of the design decisions discussed in this book to reduce error involve major allocations of resources, good questionnaire design is not much more expensive than poor questionnaire design. In the same vein, adequate and thorough pretesting, including multiple pretesting, is not a great deal more expensive than minimal pretesting, yet can yield important results if done properly.

People's sense of the error in surveys has long focused on sample design and sample size. It certainly is true that if the samples are inadequate and the response rate is poor, then investing a great deal in the design of the questions does not make sense, either. However, if one is going to invest the resources required to collect data from a good probability sample of a population, it makes little sense not to invest the effort and work it would take to generate an excellent data collection instrument.

EXERCISE

Take the questions generated in the exercise for Chapter 5 and transform them into a set of questions that an interviewer could administer in a standardized way. Pretest and revise as needed. Now put the same questions in a form for self-administration. Pretest that.

7

Survey Interviewing

Interviewers affect survey estimates in three ways: they play a major role in the response rate that is achieved, they are responsible for training and motivating respondents, and they must handle their part of the interview interaction and question-and-answer process in a standardized, nonbiasing way. This chapter discusses the significance of interviewer selection, training, and supervision, plus the procedures interviewers are given, for minimizing interviewer-related error in surveys.

OVERVIEW OF INTERVIEWER JOB

Although some surveys are carried out using self-administered forms, using interviewers to ask questions and record answers is certainly a common part of survey measurement procedures—either face to face or over the telephone.

Because of the central role they play in data collection, interviewers have a great deal of potential for influencing the quality of data they collect. The management of interviewers is a difficult task, particularly in personal interviewer studies. Furthermore, the role of the interviewer is a somewhat neglected topic in many survey texts.

For these reasons, special attention will be given to that phase of a survey research project in this chapter. The goal will be to provide an understanding of what an interviewer is supposed to do, appropriate procedures for managing interviewers, and the significance of interviewer management and performance for the quality of survey based estimates.

Interviewers have three primary roles to play in the collection of survey data:

(1) To locate and enlist the cooperation of selected respondents.
(2) To train and motivate respondents to do a good job of being a respondent.
(3) To be a good question asker and answer recorder, providing a consistent stimulus, asking questions in a standardized way, and ensuring that answers meet the question objectives.

Gaining Cooperation

Interviewers have to get in touch with respondents in order to enlist cooperation. The difficulty of that part of the job differs greatly with the sample. However, interviewers have to be available when respondents want to be interviewed, they have to be available (and persistent) enough to make contact with hard-to-reach respondents, and—for in-person interviews—they have to be able and willing to go where the respondents are.

Although many sampled individuals agree readily to be interviewed, enlisting the cooperation of uninformed or initially reluctant respondents is undoubtedly one of the hardest tasks, and one of the most important tasks, interviewers must perform. More interviewers probably fail in this area than any other.

There is no doubt that some interviewers are much better than others at enlisting cooperation. It also is clear that different personal styles will work. Some effective interviewers are very businesslike, while others are more personable. Demographic factors (age, education, gender, ethnic background) make no consistent difference. Based on experience, there are two characteristics that strong interviewers seem to share:

(1) They have a kind of confident assertiveness. They present the study as if there is no question that the respondent will want to cooperate. The tone and content of their conversation does not hint at doubt that an interview will result.

(2) They have a knack of instantly engaging people personally, so the interaction is focused on and very individually tailored to the respondent. It is not necessarily a professional interaction, but it is responsive to the individual's needs, concerns, and situation.

Although these interviewer skills are important for all surveys, they particularly are challenged by telephone surveys for which respondents receive no advance notice (as in the case when random-digit dialing is used) or when the subject matter does not readily engage respondent interest.

Training and Motivating Respondents

Respondent performance such as the accuracy of reporting has been linked to the goals they set. Interviewers have been shown to play an important role in setting respondent goals (Cannell & Fowler, 1964; Fowler, 1966). For example, interviewers who rush through interviews encourage respondents to answer questions quickly. Interviewers who read questions slowly indicate to respondents, in a nonverbal way, their willingness to take the time to obtain thoughtful, accurate answers; consequently, they obtain more accurate answers (Marquis & Cannell, 1971). Studies also show that the way interviewers provide encouragement to respondents affects their sense of what they are supposed to do and how well they report (Marquis et al., 1972; Cannell et al., 1977b).

There still is much to be learned about how interviewers motivate respondents. However, there is no doubt that most respondents have little idea of what they are expected to do, that is, how they are to perform their roles. Interviewers both explicitly and implicitly teach respondents what is expected and to varying degrees motivate them to strive for some goals, such as good, accurate reporting, and avoid others, which is an often unappreciated but critical part of the interviewer's job.

Being a Standardized Interviewer

Survey researchers would like to assume that differences in answers can be attributed to differences in the respondents themselves—that is, their views and their experiences—rather than to differences in the stimulus to which they were exposed—that is, the question, the context in which it was asked, and the way it was asked. The majority of interviewer training is aimed at teaching trainees to be standardized interviewers who do not affect the answers they obtain.

There are five aspects of interviewer behavior that researchers attempt to standardize: (1) the way they present the study and the task; (2) the way questions are asked; (3) the way inadequate answers (answers that do not meet question objectives) are probed; (4) the way answers are recorded; and (5) the way the interpersonal aspects of the interview are handled. Each of these is discussed in greater detail:

(1) *Presenting the study.* Respondents should have a common understanding of the purposes of the study, since that sense of purpose may have a bearing on the way they answer questions. Assumptions about such things as confidentiality, the voluntary nature of a project, and who will use the results also potentially can have some effect on answers. A good interviewing staff will give all respondents a similar orientation to the project so that the context of the interview is as constant as possible.

(2) *Asking the questions.* Survey questions are supposed to be asked exactly the way they are written with no variation or wording change. Even small changes in the way questions are worded have

been shown, in some instances, to have significant effects on the way questions are answered.

(3) *Probing*. If a respondent does not answer a question fully, an interviewer must ask some kind of follow-up question to elicit a better answer; that is called probing. Interviewers are supposed to probe incomplete answers in nondirective ways. By nondirective we mean probes that do not push the respondent and increase the likelihood of any one answer over another. A short list of standard probes, including repeating the question, asking "Anything else?", "Tell me more," and "How do you mean that?" will handle most situations if the questionnaire is well designed.

(4) *Recording the answers*. The recording of answers should be standardized so that no interviewer-induced variation occurs at that stage. When an open question is asked, interviewers are expected to record answers verbatim; that is, exactly in the words that the respondent uses, without paraphrasing, summarizing, or leaving anything out. In closed-response questions, when respondents are given a choice of answers, interviewers are required only to record an answer when the respondent actually chooses one. There is potential for inconsistency if interviewers code respondent words into categories that the respondent did not choose.

(5) *Interpersonal relations*. The interpersonal aspects of an interview are to be managed in a standardized way. Inevitably, an interivewer brings some obvious demographic characteristics into an interview such as gender, age, and education. However, by emphasizing the professional aspects of the interaction and focusing on the task, the personal side of the relationship can be minimized. Interviewers generally are instructed not to tell stories about themselves or express any views or opinions related to the subject matter of the interview. Interviewers are not to communicate any judgements on answers that respondents give. In short, behaviors that communicate the personal, idiosyncratic characteristics of the interviewer are to be avoided because they will vary across interviewers. To behave as a professional, not a friend, helps to standardize the relationship across interviewers and respondents.

A special complexity is introduced when the interviewer and respondent come from different backgrounds in society. In this instance, communication may not be as free and easy as when backgrounds are similiar. There is some evidence that interviewers who take steps to ease communication in such situations, by introducing a bit of humor, for example, may be able to produce a more effective interview (Fowler, 1966). However, efforts to relax the respondent should not detract from a basically professional interaction, focused on good task performance.

Significance of Interviewer's Job

It should be clear from the above that interviewing is a difficult job. Moreover, failure to perform the job may produce three different kinds of error in survey data:

(1) Samples lose credibility and are likely to be biased if interviewers do not do a good job of enlisting respondent cooperation.
(2) The precision of survey estimates will be reduced and there will be more error around estimates to the extent that interviewers are inconsistant in ways that influence the data.
(3) Answers may be systematically inaccurate or biased to the extent that interviewers fail to appropriately train and motivate respondents or fail to establish an appropriate interpersonal setting for reporting what is called for.

Given all this potential to produce error, researchers should be motivated to use "good" interviewers. There are several avenues for affecting the quality of an interviewer's work: recruitment and selection, training, supervision, and designing effective procedures. The next four sections will discuss the potential of each of these to influence interviewer performance.

INTERVIEWER RECRUITMENT AND SELECTION

Some of the characteristics of interviewers are dictated by requirements of the survey interviewer's job that have nothing to do with the quality of data per se:

(1) *Education:* Interviewers have to have reasonably good reading and writing skills. Most survey research organizations require high school graduation, and many require or prefer interviewers with at least some college experience.

(2) Interviewing is primarily *part-time, intermittent work.* It is difficult to work 40 hours a week every week on general population surveys; surveys almost always have ebbs and flows of work for interviewers. As a result, potential interviewers usually are people who can tolerate intermittent income or they are people who are

between more permanent jobs. Interviewers pay is usually not high for a college-educated person. It is unusual for a survey interviewer to be able to rely on interviewing as a primary source of income and support over a long period of time.

(3) Personal household interviewers must have some *flexibility of hours;* surveys require interviewers to be available when respondents are available. One advantage of telephone interviewing is that individual interviewers often can work more predictable shifts, although evening and weekend work is prime time for almost all general population survey work.

(4) Personal household interviewers must be *mobile,* which often excludes people with some physical disabilities and those without the use of a car. Neither of these restrictions is as salient to telephone interviewers.

As a result of the practical job requirements, the majority of survey interviewers are white, college-educated females, who have minimal child care responsibilities, unless special efforts are made to recruit other types of people.

An obvious question is whether or not criteria other than these should be applied in order to increase the likelihood of good job performance or good survey data. The answer generally is "no." Except in special cases, there is little research basis for preferring one set of candidates over others. For example,

Age. Some survey organizations avoid hiring very young adults (say, under 21). Some research suggests that data collected by very young interviewers are not as good (Sudman et al., 1974). However, those studies probably reflected the use of student interviewers used in more informal studies, with less training and supervision. Except for students, there is no proven basis for using age as a criterion for interviewer selection.

Gender. As noted, a majority of survey interviewers are female; there are more women than men in the market for part-time or sporadic work. There are people who believe that response rates by males are lower than those for females. However, there are no systematic data that show that, as a group, male interviewers have lower response rates than female interviewers.

Experience. This is not necessary. Many survey organizations prefer interviewers who have had no previous interviewer training or experience. They like to train interviewers in their own procedures and to their own standards. However, an advantage of experienced interviewers is that, as a group, they are likely to be better than new interviewers at enlisting respondent cooperation. For that reason, giving additional training to experienced interviewers, when possible, has merit.

Substantive training. The question often is raised as to whether or not some substantive training in the subject matter of a survey is helpful to an interviewer. For example, do law students make good interviewers for studies of lawyers? Are nurses or social workers particularly good interviewers for studies of health problems? There is good reason to argue just the opposite; that is, having specialized training in the subject area may be a disadvantage, because knowledgeable interviewers may assume they know what the respondent is saying when the respondent has not been clear. They may, therefore, read more into what the individual is saying than people not trained in the area. Unless interviewer observation or ratings requiring an extensive specialized background are needed, a trained interviewer with no special background usually would be the best choice.

Ethnicity. There has been a major discussion in the research literature as to whether or not it is a good idea to match interviewers and respondents on racial or ethnic backgrounds. The current thinking on this is fairly clear. For most survey topics, such matching does not affect the quality of data (NCHSR, 1977). A researcher would be best advised to send the best interviewer available to interview a respondent, regardless of ethnicity (see also Weiss, 1968).

The exception is if the subject matter of the survey directly bears on race or religion (or any demographic characteristic) and the feelings of the respondents about people in the same or different groups. For example, if people are to be interviewed about their own anti-Semitic feelings, the Jewishness of the interviewer will make a difference in the answers (Robinson & Rhode, 1946). In the same way, blacks and whites express different feelings about blacks and whites depending on the interviewer's race (Schuman & Converse, 1971).

There is no question that a researcher should consider the interaction among the subject matter and the demographic characteristics of the interviewers and respondents. Kahn and Cannell (1958) provide a good discussion of these dynamics. If ethinicity (or some other characteristic) is extremely salient to the answers to be given, some kind of matching of interviewer and respondent should be considered. However, for most surveys, the practical difficulties and costs of matching and the lack of predictable effects will argue against it.

Volunteers. Volunteer interviewing staffs are almost always unsuccessful at carrying out probability sample surveys. There are several reasons for the failure of volunteers:

(1) Since it is hard to require attendance at lengthy training sessions, usually volunteers are trained poorly.
(2) Because it is hard to terminate poor volunteer interviewers, response rates are usually low.
(3) Volunteer attrition is usually high.

Although there are exceptions to most generalizations, successful surveys are seldom carried out by volunteers.

Conclusion

The above discussion offers few guidelines for researchers in the selection of interviewers. In some rather specialized circumstances, the interviewers ethnic background, age, or gender may effect answers. For example, teenagers may respond differently to older female interviewers (Erlich & Riesman, 1961). For most surveys, however, the particular job requirements will dictate largely the pool of interviewers. There is little basis for ruling out people because of their background or personality characteristics.

Yet there clearly is a range among potential interviewers in their ability and willingness to do the interviewer's job. Almost anyone with adequate reading and writing skills can be trained to carry out the question and answer process in a reasonably effective way. The main things that differentiate successful from unsuccessful interviewers are their ability to live with the hours and pay and their ability to enlist respondent cooperation.

Unfortunately, as noted above, there is no easy way for a researcher to tell in advance which interviewers will have problems in these areas. The most feasible way to attempt to minimize interviewer attrition is to build as much information into the recruitment process as possible, in an effort to maximize the likelihood that interviewers will select themselves out before too much investment has been made in training them. Then careful monitoring during training and supervison aimed at quickly spotting problems is important. In the end, due to the difficulty of identifying good interviewers in advance, attrition of less able interviewers is probably a critical and necessary part of building a good staff of interviewers.

TRAINING INTERVIEWERS

There is great diversity in the kinds of training experiences to which survey interviewers are exposed. The exact amount of time that will be devoted to training, the kind of training session, and the content of the program obviously will depend on the particular organizational setting and what interviewers are going to be doing. There is some disagreement, in addition, on the extent to which effort should be devoted to an initial training session, prior to the onset of field experience, versus continuous learning and retraining after interviewers have begun. Nonetheless, all professional survey organizations concerned about data quality would have at least some kind of face-to-face training of all new interviewers. The following is a general summary of what reasonable interviewer training might entail. A training program available from The Survey Research Center is a good source for those interested in actually designing a training program (Guenzel et al., 1983).

Content of Training

The content of training includes both general information about interviewing that applies to all surveys and information specific to the particular study on which interviewers are to work.

The general topics to be covered will include the following:

(1) Procedures for contacting respondents and introducing the study.
(2) The conventions that are used in the design of the questionnaire with respect to wording and skip instructions so that interviewers can ask the questions in a consistent and standardized way.
(3) Procedures for probing inadequate answers in a nondirective way.
(4) Procedures for recording answers to open-ended and closed questions.
(5) Rules and guidelines for handling the interpersonal aspects of the interview in a nonbiasing way.

In addition, many research organizations feel that it is a good idea to give interviewers a sense of the way that interviewing fits into the total research process. For that reason, they often attempt to give interviewers some familiarity with sampling procedures, coding, and the kinds of analyses and reports that result from surveys. Such information may be helpful to interviewers in answering respondent questions and may play a positive role in motivating the interviewer and helping the interviewer to understand the job.

With respect to any specific project, interviewers need to know also:

(1) Specific purposes of the project, including the sponsorship, the general research goals, and anticipated uses of the research. This information is basic to providing respondents with appropriate answers to questions and helping to enlist cooperation.

(2) The specific approach that was used for sampliing, again to provide a basis for answering respondent questions. In addition, there may be some training required in how to implement the basic sample design.

(3) Details regarding the purposes of specific questions.

(4) The specific steps that will be taken with respect to confidentiality, and the kinds of assurances that are appropriate to give to respondents.

Procedures for Training

There are five basic ways to teach interviewers: written materials, lectures and presentations, planned exercises, practice role-playing, and observation of work in the field.

Written materials are usually of two types. First, it is a very good idea to have a *general interviewer manual* that provides a complete written description of interviewing procedures. In addition, for each particular study, there normally should be a *project manual*. It is tempting when interviewers are being trained in person and a project is being done in a local site to skimp on the preparation of written materials. However, newly trained interviewers say that there is an overwhelming amount of material and information to absorb during training. Having the procedures in writing enables interviewers to review material at a more leisurely pace. It also increased the odds that messages are stated clearly and accurately.

Lectures and demonstrations obviously have a role to play in any interviewer training, whether only a single interviewer is being trained or a large group of interviewers. In addition to the general presentation of required procedures and skills, most trainers find that demonstrating a standardized interview is a quick and efficient way to give interviewers a sense of how to administer an interview.

Exercises and role playing are fundamental parts of most serious interviewer training programs. Because these are new skills, supervised structured practice is one of the most important parts of interviewer training. Having interviewers take turns playing the respondent and interviewer roles is common practice.

Supervised field practice is a final strategy that many organizations consider essential. Most trainers would say the best way to do this is to have a supervisor actually accompany a trainee as an observer. In this way, the supervisor can provide the trainee with immediate evaluation and help in all aspects of the interview experience from knocking on the door to leaving the household after the interview. A less expensive alternative is to ask interviewers to tape record practice interviews.

Obviously, telephone surveys offer the potential to supervise fully practice interviews at a very low cost. Trainees who are going to work on the telephone can have their initial interview, or a practice interview, monitored totally by a supervisor. Some organizations have field interviewers do monitored practice interviews on the telephone as part of training.

Length of Training

The amount of training required will vary from study to study and setting to setting. In general, initial training for telephone interviewers is briefer than for field interviewers, in part because the work of the telephone interviewer can be supervised more closely. National field organizations, who maintain contact with interviewers primarily by mail and by phone, may be more concerned about the quality of their initial training than organizations in local settings where monitoring and retraining may be easier. Moreover, the intensity of the experinece will vary with the size of the group being trained. Two or three days one on one may be a more beneficial training experience than four or five days in a group of twenty.

With all of these differences, it is not possible to set clear standards. However, the length of formal training for a new interviewer in most academic, professional survey organizations is not less than two days and not uncommonly extends to five days. Two-day training sessions are more common in organizations that concentrate on telephone surveys. There is evidence that field interviewers trained for less than a day produce significantly more survey error than those who are trained longer (Fowler & Mangione, 1983).

SUPERVISION

The keys to good supervision are to have the information needed to evaluate interviewer performance and to invest the time and resources required to evaluate the information and provide a timely response. There are four main aspects of interviewer performance to supervise: costs, rate of response, quality of completed questionnaires, and quality of interviewing. It is considerably easier to supervise interviewers who are doing telephone interviewing from a centralized facility than those interviewing in the field.

Supervising costs for interviewers requires timely information about time spent, productivity (usually interviews completed) and (for interviewers using cars) mileage charges. It also is helpful to have a time reporting sheet that breaks down how interviewers spend their time into categories such as interviewing, editing, travel, and other administrative time.

High-cost telephone interviewers are likely to be those who work at less productive times, have high refusal rates (a refusal takes almost as much time as an interview) or who simply find ways (editing interviews, sharpening pencils) to make fewer calls per hour.

High-cost personal household interviewers are likely to live far from their sample addresses, make trips that are too short or at the wrong times (evenings and weekends are clearly the most productive), or have poor response rates.

Response rates. It is not easy to monitor response rates by interviewers on a timely basis. For a telephone study, it almost is necessary to have a computerized system recording contact results on a daily basis in order to have up-to-date cues to which interviewers are having response problems. For personal interview studies, the problem is to obtain information about refusals soon after they occur; often interviewers will "hang on" to their problems, hoping to get interviews, until a study is over and there is no chance for corrective action. Special periodic reports to supervisors of contact results usually are needed to monitor on-going rates of refusal.

Real response rates cannot be calculated until a study is over, but special efforts to identify refusals by interviewer can alert supervisors to problems and are a very important part of interviewer supervision.

It is difficult to help an interviewer who has response rate problems. On telephone studies, a supervisor can listen to introductions and provide feedback immediately after the interview (or noninterview) about how the interviewer might be more effective. For field interviewers, the task is more difficult because the supervisor cannot observe the interviewer's approach unless the supervisor accompanies the interviewer on a trip. Thus the supervisor often must be content with listening to the interviewer give a sample introduction.

Supervisors can give helpful hints to interviewers. In addition to working on the details of introductions, supervisors may need to address an interviewer's general feeling about approaching people or about the study project and its value. However, there are limits to how much retraining will help. There are people who never can attain good response rates. Although it is stressful, one of the most effective ways to keep response rates high is to take ineffective interviewers off the study.

Completed questionnaires. A sample of completed questionnaires should be reviewed to assess the quality of data interviewers are collecting. When reviewing a completed interview, one obviously can look for whether or not the recording is legible, the skip instructions are followed appropriately, and the answers obtained are complete enough to permit coding. In addition, looking at a completed interview can give a pretty good idea of the extent to which an interviewer is recording respondent answers verbatim, as compared with recording summaries or paraphrases.

The question-and-answer process cannot be supervised by reviewing completed questionnaires; that does not tell the supervisor anything at all about the way the interviewer conducted the interview and how those answers were obtained. In order to do that, a supervisor must directly observe the interviewing process.

A telephone survey from a central facility permits direct supervision of how the interviewer collects the data. A supervisor can and should be available to monitor interviewers at all times. Supervisors should listen systematically to all or parts of a sample of the interviews that each interviewer takes, evaluating, among other things: appropriate introduction of the study, asking questions exactly as written, probing appropriately and nondirectively, and appropriate handling of the interpersonal aspects of the interview. This process works best if a form rating these and other aspects of an interviewer's work is completed routinely by a monitor.

When interviewers are doing studies in respondents' homes or in other distant places, it is more difficult to supervise the question and answer process. There are only two ways to do it: A supervisor can accompany an interviewer as an observer, or interviews can be tape recorded.

Without tape recording or a program of observation, the researcher has no way to evaluate the quality of interviewing. All the most important aspects of the measurement process are unmonitored. Poor interviewers cannot be identified for retraining. The researcher cannot report the quality of interviewing beyond saying that the interviewers were told what to do. Indeed, from the interviewer's point of view, it must be difficult to believe standardized interviewing is important when it is the focus of training but not further attended to.

Although it is not yet standard practice to tape record interviews for supervisory purposes, the practice is becoming more common. There is evidence that it is a cost-effective way to reduce error in surveys (Fowler & Mangione, 1983). Cannell and associates (1975) describe effective ways to code tape recorded interviews to help supervise interviewers.

INTERVIEWING PROCEDURES

A fourth way that researchers can increase the quality of interviewer performance is by the effective design of the procedures they give interviewers to use.

The most basic thing a researcher can do is to give the interviewer a good questionnaire. Questions that are worded awkwardly are the ones that interviewers will be most apt to reword or change. If a question is well worded and easy to understand, respondents will answer directly more frequently. If respondents cannot answer a question immediately, the interviewer usually will need only to repeat a well-worded question once in order to obtain an adequate answer. The more interviewers have to probe, explain, or clarify, the more likely they are to influence answers. The better the questionnaire, the more likely it is that the interviewer will conduct a good, standardized interview.

Recent studies demonstrate the value of going beyond good question design to help standardize the interview (Cannell et al., 1977b). For example, the researcher can help the interviewer train the respondent in a consistent way. Before the interview begins, the interviewer might read something like the following:

Before we start, let me tell you a little bit about the interview process, since most people have not been in a survey like this before. You will be asked two kinds of questions in this survey. In some cases, I will be asking you to answer questions in your own words. In those cases, I will have to write down every word you say, not summarizing anything. For other questions, you will be given a set of answers, and you will be asked to choose the one that is closest to your own view. Even though none of the answers may fit your ideas exactly, choosing the response closest to your views will enable us to compare your answers more easily with those of other people.

Interestingly, interviewers like this instruction a great deal. It explains the respondents' task to them. It makes the question-and-answer process go more smoothly. In fact, good interviewers give instructions such as these on their own. The value of providing explicit instructions is that it reduces differences between interviewers by having them all do the same thing.

In addition, such instructions have a salutory effect on the interviewer's performance. Once the interviewer has read an instruction explaining the job expectations, it is easier to do the job the way it should be done, and it is a little harder to do it wrong, because the respondent now also knows what the interviewer is supposed to do.

Standardized instructions to respondents also can be used to set goals and standards for performance:

It is very important that you answer as accurately as you can. Take your time. Consult records if you want. Ask me to clarify if you have any question about what is wanted.

Such statements ensure that repondents have a common understanding of their priorities. Some interviewers unintentionally promise respondents they will make it easy on respondents if they will just give the interview; interviewers who hurry communicate that speed is more important than accuracy. When an instruction such as the above is read, it forces accuracy and data quality to be a central part of the role expectations for both respondent and interviewer. One more source of inter-interviewer variability is reduced, and the odds of good performance by both are increased.

Cannell and associates (1977b) tried an even stronger approach, requiring respondents to sign a form committing themselves to "try their best to give accurate and complete information" before they were "allowed" to be interviewed. Numerous refusals were expected, but did not occur. Response rates were unaffected by the form, while reporting was improved.

Cannell also has tried to standardize the reinforcement interviewers give to respondents. Interviewers often inadvertently reinforce undesirable respondent behaviors (e.g., quick, thoughtless answers). When Cannell and associates (1977b) designed interview schedules that forced interviewers to praise good behavior (e.g., checking records or answering slowly), respondent reporting improved. Using such procedures is somewhat difficult on a routine basis, but the work emphasizes the need to minimize inappropriate reinforcement by interviewers.

In conclusion, there are critical parts of the interviewer's job besides the direct question and answer process. In particular, the interviewer is responsible for communicating to the respondent how the interview is to proceed: what the respondent is supposed to do, what the interviewer is going to do, and what their joint goals are. This aspect of the interviewer's job mainly has been left up to the interviewer, and, not surprisingly, interviewers differ as to how they do it—in ways that affect data. By developing standardized instruction programs for respondents, researchers can make the job of the interviewer easier, reduce an important source of between-interviewer variance, and improve the extent to which interviewers and respondents behave in ways that will make the measurement process go better.

VALIDATION

Every survey organization worries about the possibility that an interviewer will "make up" an interview. The likelihood of this happening varies with the sample, the interviewing staff, and the field procedures. For the most part, concern about validation is restricted to surveys in which interviewers are asked to interview respondents in their homes. In such cases, the actual collection of data is not observable. The number of hours to be devoted to carrying out an interview is often sufficient to motivate an interviewer to make up an interview rather than take the time and effort to carry it out.

In the long run, probably the best protection against "faked" interviews is to have a set of interviewers that has some commitment to the quality of the research and the organization. Such problems seem to occur most often with newly hired interviewers. However, even organizations with an experienced, professional staff routinely check a sample of interviews to make sure they were taken.

TABLE 7.1
Multipliers of Estimates of Standard Errors of Means Due to Interviewer Effects* for Selected Values of Rho and Average Interviewer Assignments

Average Interviewer Assignment	Intraclass Correlation (Rho)				
	.005	.01	.015	.02	.03
11	1.002	1.05	1.07	1.10	1.14
21	1.05	1.10	1.14	1.18	1.26
31	1.07	1.14	1.20	1.26	1.38
51	1.12	1.22	1.32	1.41	1.58
81	1.18	1.34	1.48	1.61	1.84
101	1.22	1.41	1.58	1.73	2.00

*Estimates of standard errors calculated from the sample size and design should be inflated by the multiplier in the table to take into account the effect of interviewers.

There are two approaches to so-called validation. One approach is to mail respondents a brief, follow-up questionnaire asking about reactions to the interview. Probably a more common procedure is to have interviewers obtain a telephone number from every respondent; a sample is called by a supervisor.

Simply knowing in advance that a validation—by mail or telephone—will be done is likely to be a deterrent to interviewer cheating. In addition, to be able to say that such a check was done may be reassuring to users of the data.

THE ROLE OF DATA COLLECTION IN SURVEY ERROR

As noted at the onset of this chapter, interviewers affect response rates, the accuracy of reporting, and the consistency or precision of measurement. Each of these has a central role in the quality of a survey estimate.

One of the most observable effects of good survey management is the response rate. Although that issue is discussed more thoroughly in Chapter 3, it is worth repeating that the quality of an interviewing staff has a critical role in the rate of response that will be obtained in any particular survey.

It is more difficult to measure the error introduced by interviewers in the question-and-answer process. Often survey error is undetectable. When asking questions about subjective states, objective checks for bias or inaccuracy are generally not feasible, as was discussed Chapter 5. There have been studies, however, in which researchers had objective measures of facts respondents were asked to report, permitting evaluation of the accuracy of reporting. In one such study (Cannell et al., 1977a), samples of households in which someone had been hospitalized in the year preceding were interviewed. The accuracy of reporting could be evaluated by comparing the health interview reports of hospital stays with hospital records. One measure of reporting accuracy was simply the percentage of known hospitalizations that was reported.

In this study, it was found that the number of interviews assigned to an interviewer correlated very highly ($r = .72$) with the percentage of hospitalizations that were unreported in the interview. Interviewers who had large assignments, with whatever pressures that brought to bear on them, were not as good as those with small assignments.

A different study using the same criterion (the percentage of hospitalizations reported, Cannell & Fowler, 1964) reached a similar conclusion. In this case, half of an interviewer's respondents reported hospitalizations in an interview, while the other half completed a self-administered form regarding hospitalizations after the interviewer had completed the rest of the health interview. It was found that interviewers whose respondents reported with great accuracy when asked to report hospitalizations in the interview also had respondents who reported very well in the self-administered form after the interviewer had left ($r = .65$). This study suggested not only that interviewers had a critical role to play in affecting the error of their respondents' reporting, but also that one way in which interviewers affected respondent performance was the degree to which they motivated respondents to perform well. In both cases, the effect of the interviewer on reporting accuracy was clear.

In the absence of validating data, one cannot assess accuracy but can assess the extent to which interviewers influence the answers of their respondents. If an interviewing staff were operating in a perfectly standardized way, one would be unable to explain any variation in answers by knowing who the interviewer was. To the extent that answers are predictable, in part, from knowing who did the interview, it can be concluded that the interviewer is inappropriately influencing answers.

It turns out that for many questions that interviewers ask, one cannot see any effect of the interviewer. For about a third of the questions that are asked in most surveys, however, interviewers have been found to account for 1 percent or more of the total variance in answers; for about 10 percent of items, interviewers can be associated with more than 2 percent of the variance (see Groves & Kahn, 1979).

The result of these interviewer effects is to increase the standard errors around survey estimates. The size of the multiplier depends on the size of the intraclass correlation (rho) and on the average size of an interviewers assignments (see Kish, 1962; Groves & Magilavy, 1980). Table 7.1 puts these two numbers together to show the importance of interviewer effects on the precision of survey estimates. If the intraclass correlation is .01, and the average interviewer assignment is about 31, the standard errors of means will be increased by 14 percent over those estimated from the sample design alone. When interviewer assignments average closer to 50, for items with an intraclass correlation of .02, the estimates of standard errors will be increased by 41 percent.

Out of this discussion there are several points to be made about the role of the interviewer in the total-error structure of survey data.

(1) In addition to their role in response rates, interviewers can be associated with the extent to which respondents given inaccurate answers in surveys and with measurement inconsistency. Although there is much work to be done to document the extent of such errors and the conditions under which they are greatest, existing evidence clearly indicates that interviewers are a significant source of error for many kinds of measures.

(2) The training and supervision that interviewers receive can significantly increase the consistency of interviewers, thereby improving the reliability of estimates, and reduce bias. In particular, interviewers who receive minimal training (e.g., less than a day) and interviewers who receive minimal feedback about the quality of their interviewing, are less good interviewers.

(3) Procedures that structure the training and instruction of respondents, minimize inappropriate interviewer feedback, and, in general, control more of the interviewer's behavior can reduce interviewer effects on data and increase overall accuracy.

(4) Probably better question design also will reduce interviewer effects.

(5) One design option that has been unappreciated is the size of the average interviewer assignment. Although training and management costs may be lower if a smaller number of interviewers is used, researchers may pay a price in data reliability for allowing individual interviewers to take large numbers of interviews. Reducing average interviewer assignments is a cost-effective way to increase the precision of survey estimates.

(6) Virtually all reports of the reliability of survey estimates ignore the effects of interviewers on data. In part, this is because researchers cannot sort out interviewer effects from sampling effects when interviewers are assigned samples on a nonrandom basis, such as convenience or geographic proximity. However, interviewer effects are a significant source of variance for up to 30 percent of the items in most surveys. Although, we do not have now a good profile of which items are most susceptible to interviewer effects, any report of the precision of a survey estimate that ignores interviewer effects is likely to be an underestimate of survey error.

In conclusion, the role of the interviewer in contributing to error in survey data has not been appreciated generally. Although most survey researchers know that some training is necessary for interviewers, procedures for training and supervising interviewers vary widely and often are not adequate. It is unusual for researchers to make any efforts beyond training and supervision to minimize interviewer effects. Yet, these aspects of survey design constitute some of the most cost-effective ways to improve the quality of survey data. More important, the effect of interviewers on estimates seldom is considered in reports of the precision of survey estimates. The impact of the interviewer on survey estimates deserves a central place in the design and reporting of survey studies that it has not yet achieved.

EXERCISE

Tape-record some role played interviews in which you and/or others use a standardized interview schedule (the questions developed in Chapter 6 or a schedule from another source). Then listen to the tapes and systematically evaluate interviewer performance by noting for each question a least the following errors: did not read question exactly as worded; probed an inadequate answer in a biasing (directive) way; failed to probe an unclear answer; and other possibly biasing or undstandardized interpersonal behavior. The evaluations are particularly instructive if done by a group, so inteviewer errors can be discussed.

8

Preparing Survey Data for Analysis

Survey answers usually must be transformed into data files for computer analysis. This chapter describes options and good practice for data formats, code development, coding procedures and management, data entry, and data checking procedures.

Once data have been collected by survey, no matter what the methods, they almost invariably must be translated into a form appropriate for computer analysis. This chapter is about the process of taking completed questionnaires and survey interviews and preparing them for analysis.

The process of coding or data reduction in the survey involves five separate phases:

(1) Formatting or organizing the data.
(2) Designing the code—that is, the rules by which a respondent's answers will be assigned numerical values.
(3) Coding—that is, the process of turning responses into numbers.
(4) Data entry—that is, keying the numbers onto cards, tapes, or disks so the computers can read them.
(5) Data cleaning—that is, doing a final check on the data file for accuracy and consistency prior to the onset of analysis.

We will discuss each of those aspects of the data reduction process in turn.

FORMATTING A DATA FILE

Each computing facility has its own local conventions regarding how data should be formatted. The following are some common principles:

(1) Even if actual data cards are not to be used, a card-and-column format for specifying the location of data is very common.

(2) Identifying information—a serial identifier for each respondent, plus card and project identification—usually goes at the front (in the early columns) of the code for each card.

(3) If data are to be coded from a questionnaire, it eases coding, keypunching, and programmer tasks if the data are coded in order.

(4) Multiple punches in a single column are acceptable to some programs, not to others. It probably is best to avoid them.

CONSTRUCTING A CODE

A code is a set of rules that translates answers into numbers and vice versa. Which numbers go with which answers is irrelevant to the computer. However, it aids reliable coding and appropriate interpretation of data that the code be unambiguous. There should be a clear rule for what number to assign to each and every answer (or other result). In addition, codes can be designed to minimize errors during coding and analysis. The following are some common principles:

(1) Be sure to have codes for missing data (i.e., questions that are not answered). Codes should differentiate between

   (a) *Not ascertained* information, where codable information was not obtained due to poor interviewer or respondent performance; some researchers also like a separate code to differentiate respondent refusals to answer a question from questions unanswered for other reasons.

   (b) *Inapplicable* information, where the information does not apply to a particular respondent (e.g., length of hospitalization for those not hospitalized).

   (c) *"Don't know"* answers may be treated as "not ascertained" or as a meaningful response, depending on the question and the researcher's goals.

Do not use blanks to indicate missing data because many computers read them as zeros.

(2) Be consistent in assigning numbers; always use the same code for "not ascertained" or "don't know" responses. The more consistent the code, the fewer errors coders and programmers will make.

(3) Make codes fit numbers in the real world when possible. Code numbers exactly (e.g., code a 45-year-old person as "45"). Also

number a list of responses in the order they appear on the questionnaire, if there is no compelling reason to do otherwise.

When response alternatives are provided to respondents or the response form is highly structured, the code constructor's job simply is to assign numbers to the predictable set of answers and account for missing data. However, when respondents are asked to answer questions in their own words, the range of answers will not be fully predictable. In this case, rather than assigning numbers to a known set of responses, there is an interactive process whereby the researcher lets categories emerge from the answers as well as imposing order on the answers that are obtained.

In order to construct such a code:

(1) Have a clear idea about what characteristics of answers are of analytic significance. A good first step is to jot down the kinds of differences among answers that are important from the researcher's point of view.

(2) Actually tabulate some of the answers from early interviews. Then construct a draft code for classifying those answers.

(3) Try the classification scheme on another 10 or 20 interviews; revise as needed.

(4) Have a separate code for "other" responses that do not fit the categories clearly and have coders make out cards recording the "other" answers. Those cards can be used to expand and clarify the code or add needed categories as well as providing a record of answers not captured in the code.

(5) The same kind of card system should be used to allow coders to communicate problems or ambiguities to the researcher, who in turn should refine the definitions and policies.

These steps, together with an effective check coding operation (discussed below) should produce an exhaustive and nonoverlapping categorization system, that unambiguously puts each answer into one and only one place and that can be shared by coders, coding supervisors, and researchers who will analyze the data.

APPROACHES TO DATA ENTRY

In the 1960s and before, coders transcribed code numbers onto special coding sheets. The numbers thus recorded then were punched onto IBM cards.

In recent years, there has been a major shift in the way that the data reduction process is handled. Most survey instruments are set up for "direct keypunching." The questionnaire itself almost becomes a codebook. The card and column locations where the answers will be recorded are printed right on the survey instrument. Fixed alternative responses are numbered on the questionnaire. The data enterer uses the completed survey instrument as the source.

This change does not eliminate the need for a coder. Researchers generally do not like the keypunchers to make substantive decisions about what to enter. As a result, trained coders or editors go through completed questionnaires to make sure that what is to be punched for each question is completely clear; editors write in codes for skipped questions or questions where inadequate or ambiguous answers were obtained.

In addition, such editors/coders will code any question that is answered in an open form by simply writing the appropriate number code in the questionnaire.

There are three disadvantages to having entered data directly from edited questionnaires:

(1) It takes longer to enter from completed questionnaires than from a specially prepared coding sheet.

(2) Certain kinds of checks that one can do from a standard coding sheet are difficult to do from completed questionnaires. For example, when coding open questions, one might decide to revise a particular code category in process. From coding sheets, it is a simple task to find all the interviews where a particular code was used and check the consistency of coding. When the source is a completed questionnaire, it is virtually impossible; checking would have to occur only after data entry.

(3) Independent check coding of coders is more difficult when coders are writing their codes on the questionnaire. Prior to actual coding, a check coder must record codes on a separate sheet in order for checking to be independent.

These disadvantages usually are outweighed by the advantages. Simple transcription errors virtually are eliminated. Moreover, the process is cheaper for most studies, since the majority of survey questions are closed and hence precoded.

If an interview schedule has a very high percentage of open questions, the improved check coding and modest, cost differential might make a researcher consider coding onto standard coding sheets rather than direct data entry. However, for most social science surveys, direct data entry from a completed survey form is the method of choice.

KEYPUNCHING CARDS VERSUS
DIRECT DATA ENTRY

The IBM data card has been a standard part of the data reduction process in survey research for many years. The card itself plays an intermediary role in the data reduction process. Most computers also take data input from tapes or data stored on disks. Cards only are used once, for the most part, to be read onto a tape or disk.

Cards have maintained their place in the survey research world mainly because the equipment exists in many places to enter data onto cards, but not onto tapes or disks directly. This is changing rapidly, however.

Entering data directly onto a tape has some advantages besides avoiding cards. Checks for legal codes and for internal consistency can be done at the time of data entry. That capability does not exist on card keypunching machines. Thus the time required to produce a "clean" data file can be reduced.

The extreme case of reducing the number of participants in the data entry process is Computer Assisted Telephone Interviewing (CATI) systems. For telephone surveys, survey instruments have been programmed on computers. Interviewers read the questions off a screen and enter answers directly into a terminal. The answers to open-ended questions either are recorded onto a paper form or they are typed verbatim into the computer for later coding.

Such systems are definitely in the experimental stages in 1984, though there are many surveys carried out using these systems. So far such procedures are not problem free. For a complex, one-time survey, a good deal of programming is required prior to the beginning of field work. "Bugs" and problems with the computer systems are common and are particularly troublesome when they crop up in the middle of an interview. However, one of the coming changes in survey research will be increased use of systems that permit interviewers to enter data directly.

VERIFICATION

When data are entered onto cards or tape, it is good practice to key verify all the data entry; that is, to have another person independently enter the data, with a process that checks the second entry against the initial one. Although much data entry is done with a high degree of accuracy, it can be done poorly, too. Verification is not expensive in the context of most overall survey budgets, and it virtually eliminates error due to data entry.

A price of having interviewers enter data directly, if no hard copy of answers is made, is that there is no chance to measure or correct data entry errors.

CODER MANAGEMENT

The characteristics required of a good coder are virtually opposite from those one would look for in an interviewer. Obviously, interpersonal skills are of minimal importance; good conceptual skills are very important. Appearance is irrelevant; concentration and attention to detail are paramount.

Although it is difficult to tell a good coder in advance, finding good coders is not difficult. Coding is an excellent part-time job for students. The talents that make good students are often those that make good coders.

Training coders consists of two separate steps. First, they need to be familiarized with general principles of coding and formatting data: the consistent conventions that are going to be used in coding and the rules for coding open questions. Then for every study, there should be a training session devoted specifically to what the interviewers were supposed to do and what the specific coding rules are going to be.

Unless it is the simplest of coding tasks, almost certainly the code itself will undergo some refinement during the coding process. A researcher cannot anticipate every contingency coders will encounter. Inevitably some code categories initially will be poorly defined. Thus the management of the coding process must be geared to two things: (1) finding the problems as quickly as possible; and (2) ensuring that policy solutions to those problems are applied consistently.

There are three basic ways to manage properly the coding process. First, it is important that a sample of all coded work be check coded independently. Second, coders should fill out a card for the supervisor every time they are faced with a coding decision for which, in their view, the rules for decision making are not clear. Third, a "code change and policy book" is needed to ensure consistent dissemination of policies. Whenever a refinement or change in coding policy is made, it should be entered in a central book. Coders should be required to check that book each day before they begin production coding.

After coding is completed, a final code book for use in analysis should be compiled that incorporates the various refinements, amendments, and policies that emerged during the coding process. In addition, it is good practice to calculate the rate of disagreement found in the check coding of each variable. These figures may be appended to the code book or, more simply, codes that proved particularly troublesome should be flagged to warn users of the data.

DATA CLEANING

Once interviews have been coded and the data entered onto a tape or disk file, the data need to be checked. First, every field should be checked to make sure that only legal codes occur. Second, data files should be checked for inconsistent data. Statements in the form of "If X is true and Y is not true, identify the case" are useful for finding such inconsistencies.

Researchers have discretion in deciding the extent to which they want to perform consistency checks beyond those that necessarily are implied by the data format. Some researchers do very little checking for consistency, preferring to have footnotes saying occasional inconsistencies will occur. Others perform all conceivable checks. To a certain extent, decisions like that are a matter of taste and aesthetics as well as budget and time rather than data quality.

CODING AND DATA REDUCTION AS SOURCES OF ERRORS IN SURVEYS

Because coding and data reduction take place in a highly supervised setting and have the capability of being checked thoroughly, there is the potential to have it be an almost error-free part of the survey process. Moreover, the costs of coding and data reduction usually are a small fraction of the total survey cost.

When dealing with closed answers, the rate of error associated even with transcribing the number onto a coding sheet should be considerably less than 1 percent in a well-run coding operation. The level of error will be lower, of course, when those numbers are entered and verified directly.

The reliability of coding open-opinion responses will vary with the quality of the question and the quality of the code. If a researcher has a reasonably focused question and if code categories are conceptually clear, one should expect coding to exceed 90 percent in reliability; that is, the coder and check coder will disagree in the classification of fewer than one out of ten answers. Coders that are not trained and check coded appropriately can create errors at considerably higher rates. Codes that depend on knowing complex definitions such as occupational categories, health conditions, or specific crimes may warrant special attention to coder training and check coding.

The process of data entry can be error free if it is verified. Although some individual operators are able to enter data at a remarkable level of accuracy, with error rates below 1 in 1000, one cannot assume routinely that data entry will occur at that level of competence. Moreover, knowledge of verification is likely to improve the care with which data entry is done.

Finally, the value of data cleaning can be debated. If coding and data entry have been handled well, researchers find few errors at the stage of data cleaning. Most researchers find that it is aesthetically pleasing and professional to check for legal codes and obvious inconsistencies. However, the value of that for actually affecting the quality of survey estimates usually is minimal. Basically, the key steps to good data are having a well-constructed questionnaire, well-constructed codes, well-trained coders who are check coded, and verification of data entry.

9

Ethical Issues in Survey Research

Like all social research, surveys should be carried out in ways designed to avoid risks to participants, respondents and interviewers. This chapter summarizes procedures for ethically managing surveys.

Like all research that involves human subjects, the survey researcher needs to be attentive to the ethical manner in which the research is carried out. A basic guideline is that the researcher should make sure that no individual suffers any adverse consequences as a result of the survey. Moreover, to the extent that it is feasible, a good researcher also will be attentive to maximizing positive outcomes of the research process.

In this text, it is not possible to address all the issues that may be involved in studies of special populations. Research on children, the mentally retarded, the mentally ill, prisoners, and other special populations may require attention for which researchers may get guidance elsewhere. The following, however, are some ethical principles about doing surveys of general populations with which all survey researchers should be familiar.

INFORMING RESPONDENTS

The survey research process generally involves enlisting voluntary cooperation. It is a basic premise of ethical survey research that respondents should be informed about what it is that they are volunteering for. Respondents should have the following information before being asked to answer questions:

(1) The name of the organization that is carrying out the research. If an interviewer is involved, the respondent also should have the interviewer's name.

(2) The sponsorship, that is, who is supporting or paying for the research.
(3) A reasonably accurate, though brief, description of the purposes of the research. Is the research trying to increase general or basic knowledge or is there some planning or action process that the research is designed to assist? What issues or topics is the research designed to cover?
(4) An accurate statement of the extent to which answers are protected with respect to confidentiality. If there are risks to or limits on the confidentiality that is being offered, they should be clearly stated.
(5) Assurance that cooperation is voluntary and that no negative consequences will result to those who decide not to participate in the survey study.
(6) Assurance that respondents can skip any questions that they do not want to answer.

This information may be mailed in advance or given directly to respondents, if the design permits. However, regardless of what else is done, interviewers (if they are used) should be required to review the above points with respondents before beginning an interview.

Finally, perhaps a word is appropriate about signed consent forms. Generally speaking, respondents to sample surveys are not asked to sign forms prior to completing an interview. Obviously, it is not feasible to obtain signed forms on telephone surveys. However, even in personal interview surveys, most thoughtful review committees feel that signed consent forms are not needed. In most cases, the risks involved in participation in surveys are quite minimal and well under the control of the researcher. In addition, respondents have an opportunity to reexercise their decision to participate in a survey every time a new question is asked.

The only time a consent form might seem appropriate would be if people were asked to provide information that, in fact, could produce harm to them if it were misused or if there were limits to the protection being offered. In those cases, the researcher might feel protected if a piece of paper was signed by respondents that acknowledged an appreciation of the kind of data that would be asked for and any limits that might exist to the protection of that information.

PROTECTING RESPONDENTS

The main issue with respect to protecting respondents is the way in which the information they provide will be treated. Some standard procedures that careful survey researchers take to minimize the chances of a breach of confidentiality are:

(1) All people who have access to the data or a role in the data collection should be committed in writing to confidentiality.

(2) Minimize links between answers and identifiers. Names or addresses are the most common identifiers. Often names are not required in order to execute a proper survey. When they can be avoided, many survey organizations do not use names in any part of the research process. When there are specific identifiers such as names or addresses, they are put on pieces of paper (or coversheets) that can be separated physically from the interview schedule in which the actual survey responses are recorded.

(3) Completed interview schedules should not be accessible to non-project members.

(4) Identifiers should be removed from completed questionnaires if nonstaff people are going to look at them; it is common to remove them as soon as possible in any case.

(5) Individuals who could identify respondents from their profile of answers, such as supervisors in the case of a survey of employees or teachers in the case of a survey of students, should not be permitted to see the actual questionnaire responses.

(6) The actual data files usually will have some kind of an ID number for each respondent. The link between the ID number and the sample addresses or the identifiers should not be available to general users of the data file.[1]

(7) During analysis, researchers should be careful about presenting data for very small categories of people who might be identifiable.

(8) When a project is completed, or when use of the actual survey questionnaires is over, it is the responsibility of the researcher to see to the eventual destruction of completed survey research instruments, or their continuing secure storage.

Obviously, deviation from these particular procedures may be required for a given project. However, the general approach and concerns reflected in this set of procedures should typify any responsible survey research project.

BENEFITS TO RESPONDENTS

In most surveys, the main benefits to respondents are intrinsic: enjoying the process of the interview or feeling they contributed to a worthwhile effort. More direct benefits—payment, prizes, services—are sometimes provided. When services are offered, attention must be paid to providing them in a way that does not compromise the promised confidentiality of the survey answers. Other than that, the key ethical responsibility is to be certain not to overstate the benefits and to deliver the benefits promised. In particular, the researcher who enlists cooperation by describing the uses of the research assumes a commitment to ensure appropriate analysis and dissemination of the data.

ETHICAL RESPONSIBILITIES TO INTERVIEWERS

Beyond the obligations of any employer, the researcher has responsibilities to interviewers in two areas. First, the interviewer is given the responsibility of presenting the research to the respondents. It is the researcher's obligation to make sure that interviewers have full and accurate information to give about the research. The researcher should not put the interviewer in a position of being deceptive, misleading, or inaccurate.

Second, the researcher must deal with interviewer safety and fear of crime. Because samples will include all areas, interviewers may have to visit neighborhoods in which they do not feel safe. The following guidelines may be helpful.

(1) Interviewers legitimately can be asked to visit sample addresses in a car before deciding they do not feel safe. Neighborhood areas are heterogeneous and vary from block to block.
(2) Interviewers should be told explicitly that it is not a job requirement to go somewhere under circumstances that they feel unsafe. Options include avoiding night calls, using weekend days to interview employed people, and interviewing with another interviewer or paid escort. A good approach is to ask interviewers to work with the field supervisor to figure out how to carry out interviews in a way that feels safe.
(3) Interviewers should be briefed on sensible procedures to reduce the risks of their being victims.

Fortunately, victimization is rare; fear is more the problem. However, in our society, crimes do occur. Both researchers and interviewers need to feel that interviewers were informed and were not encouraged to go anywhere or to do anything that would increase the real likelihood that they would be a victim of a crime.

CONCLUSION

The ethical issues in survey research are not different from those in the social sciences in general. The real risks and potential costs of being a respondent (or interviewer) in most surveys are minimal. However, certain basic steps are needed to reduce whatever risks there are either to participants or to the image of social science researchers. The specific steps outlined above are by no means exhaustive. The basic approach of dealing with everyone in an honest way, however, with continuing attention to the details that will maximize benefits and avoid costs, should be an integral part of any survey research effort.

NOTE

1. Questionnaires can be subpoenaed by a court. Researchers can protect themselves from this threat to promised confidentiality in several ways. If research involves especially sensitive material—such as drug or criminal justice studies might entail—researchers can petition federal or state agencies for protection from subpoena. Alternatively, concerned researchers simply may destroy the link between identifiers and responses.

10

Providing Information About Survey Methods

Researchers reporting survey estimates have a scientific obligation to provide a full description of the details of the procedures they used that could affect those estimates. In addition, they should perform and report calculations relevant to the precision and accuracy of their figures. This chapter discusses the material that should be included in a full methodological description of a survey.

There are few methodological decisions that a researcher could make that could be labeled categorically as "wrong." There are some research situations in which any of the compromises discussed in this book might be appropriate and cost effective for gathering information.

Although research design decisions cannot be criticized out of context, the failure to describe procedures fully by which data were collected can be criticized without exception. It is essential for readers and users of survey data to have access to a full and complete description of the data collection process.

There are two general functions of a good methodological description:

(1) To provide a good understanding of how well sample estimates are likely to describe the population from which the sample was drawn. It is not enough simply to state the author's conclusions on this matter; detailed calculations relevant to precision and bias should be presented that will permit readers to make their own assessments.

(2) To provide the procedural details needed to replicate a data collection effort and/or detect procedural differences between surveys that would affect comparability.

It is not unusual to find only the sample size reported about a survey; more conscientious researchers will include a description of their sampling strategies and response rates. Although the appropriate level of detail will vary with the way the data are being used, the following is a brief outline of information that should be provided about any survey.

(1) The sample frame (i.e., those people from whom the sample was drawn) together with an estimate of the percentage of the population studied that had a chance of selection from that frame and anything that is known about the way in which the excluded people differ from the population as a whole.

(2) The sampling procedure, including any deviations from simple random sampling such as clustering, stratification, or unequal rates of selection among subgroups of the population.

(3) Field results, the disposition of the initially designated sample, which describes the number of respondents, the number of nonresponses, and the major reasons for nonresponse. A description of the field procedures used to enlist cooperation, including strategies for the follow-up of nonrespondents, should be included in this section to help the reader appreciate how the rate of response came about. If the rate of response cannot be calculated exactly because the sample frame included ineligible units (such as telephone numbers not associated with occupied housing units), the researcher should report the number of units for which eligibility was not ascertained and an estimate of the most likely response rate.

(4) A description of who carried out the interviewing, if interviewers were used: their demographic characteristics, something about their previous experience, the kind of training that they had, and the supervisory procedures that were used during data collection.

(5) A brief description of questionnaire design procedures, including any pretesting that was done and the kind of evaluation that was done of the pretest.

(6) The exact wording of questions analyzed, if they are not reproduced in the text. For a major report, the entire questionnaire should be reproduced.

(7) The quality control and checking procedures that were used during coding, data entry, and preparing the data file for analysis.

In addition to factual description of the data collection process, there are five other "desiderata" in a methodological appendix.

First, most reports are intended for audiences that go beyond survey research methodologists. Therefore, a brief overview of the possible kinds of error in surveys usually is an appropriate introduction to a methodological section on a survey.

Second, numerical estimates of the amount of sampling error associated with the particular design of the sample should be included. If the sample design was stratified and clustered or if different rates of selection were used, the effects of those design features will be different for different measures in the survey. Typically, researchers calculate these "design effects" for a number of measures in the survey, including some they expect to be most and least affected by the sample design. They then either present the design effects for these items or report the range of the design effects, with some generalizations about the kinds of items that are affected most by the sample design. A generalized table such as that found in Chapter 2, which presents estimates of average sampling errors for samples of different sizes around different proportions, is also a common aid to readers.

Third, researchers who carry out telephone surveys from a central facility are able to make a reasonable calculation of the extent to which interviewers affect answers. Such calculations are rare in the literature to date. However, there is a growing set of studies that gives a range of interviewer effects (e.g., Groves & Kahn, 1979). At the very least, a researcher should report the number of interviews on the average that an interviewer took and estimate for readers how much the interviewer effects might inflate the confidence intervals beyond those calculated for the sample design alone.

Fourth, a researcher should tell readers as much as is known about the effect of nonresponse on sample estimates. If the researcher sampled from a source that provides information about those for whom interviews were not obtained, that information can be presented. Interviewers should be encouraged to get at least some information about people who refuse, so the researcher can say something about ways nonrespondents may differ from respondents. Finally, if there are statistics from other sources about the population from which the sample was drawn, such as relatively recent Census figures, the researcher can compare the sample with such independent aggregate figures to estimate some effects of nonresponse on the sample.

Finally, a good methodological appendix should include some information about the reliability and validity of the major measures used in a survey. If the researcher is measuring a subjective state, relevant correlations with other measures should be presented. For measures of factual behaviors, a researcher should report what the methodological literature has to say about how well people report what has been measured. The researcher also should present patterns of association that would help convince the reader that the measures are orderly and measure what they are supposed to measure.

There will be reports of survey data for which all the information outlined above would be too detailed. However, all of the information is decidely relevant to assessment of the likely quality of a survey-based estimate. In a full report of a survey analysis, a full methodological appendix such as this should be included. When shorter works are published, a methodological report covering the details of the data collection process at least should be available on request.

EXERCISE

Using the standards presented in this chapter, systematically evalulate the adequacy and completeness of the methodological section of a published book or report that was based on survey.

11

Survey Error in Perspective

The cost of trying to achieve error-free estimates is too high for most research purposes; some potential for error exists in virtually all survey plans. Total survey design involves considering all aspects of a survey and choosing a level of rigor appropriate to the particular project purposes. The most common deviations from good survey design and practice are discussed in this chapter, together with an assessment of their cost-saving potential and their significance for the precision, accuracy, and credibility of survey estimates.

THE CONCEPT OF TOTAL SURVEY DESIGN

Any reader of the text to this point should have a good sense of what total survey design means. The collection of data by sample survey involves numerous steps. There are decisions to be made about how each of these steps will be carried out. Those decisions have implications for the accuracy and credibility of the data. Total survey design means that when one is designing a survey or evaluating the quality of survey data, one looks at the complete data collection process, not simply at one or two aspects of the survey. The quality of the sample (the frame, the size, the design, the response rate), the quality of the questions as measures, the quality of data collection (especially the use of effective training and supervising procedures), and the mode of data collection constitute a tightly interrelated set of issues and design decisions.

The full appreciation of the total survey design approach to survey error has three concrete implications:

(1) In designing a survey data collection, the researcher self-consciously takes into account tradeoffs between costs and methodological rigor in all aspects of the survey design process. Investments in error reduction in one aspect of the survey are not made when other aspects of the survey do not warrant that kind of investment.

(2) In evaluating the quality of data, researchers ask questions about how all of the decisions affecting data quality were made and carried out.

(3) In reporting the details of a survey, a researcher will report relevant details of all aspects of the data collection effort that impinge on the error of the data.

ERROR IN PERSPECTIVE

It is difficult to generalize across all projects regarding the significance of the various methodological choices discussed in this book. The cost of making the rigorous decision varies a great deal across choices as well as varying from research situation to situation. In the same way, the potential for error from making the less costly decision also varies greatly. The notion of a custom design for a survey means that a researcher should go down the list of design options carefully, assess the alternatives, assess the cost potential for error, and make decisions about which compromises make sense and which do not. The following are some generalizations that can be made that may be helpful, however.

In fact, it is fairly rare to have a perfect *sample frame* that gives every member of the population that the researcher wants to study a known chance of selection. Whom to sample truly is a decision that cannot be evaluated out of context. However, it is incumbent on researchers to be very clear about how comprehensive their sample frame was, who was omitted, and not imply that their sample estimates apply to people who had no chance to be sampled.

Probably the most common cost-saving compromise in survey research occurs in the sampling area. At worst, people try to generalize from data collected from people who were not sampled at all, such as magazine readers who voluntarily fill out questionnaires. However, using *nonprobability samples,* substituting more available or willing people for those more difficult to enlist in a sample, is standard practice for many well-known polling firms; it is typical of most public opinion, political, and market research. In fact for telephone surveys, permitting sample substitution does not save a great deal of money, though it does permit doing surveys quickly. However, for household interviews in person, there is a considerable cost difference between probability and nonprobability samples. The major price one pays for such cost savings is to give up statistical credibility with respect to the error in the data; there is no scientific basis for describing the relationship of the sample to the population sampled. If the goal of a survey is to solicit the views of a broader spectrum of the population than would be readily at hand in some other way, such nonstatistical sampling procedures may serve the purpose well. However, if more than order of magnitude estimates are of interest and when scientific credibility is an issue, the cost savings derived from sample substitution probably are not worth it.

A nearly equally common compromise in surveys is to accept *low response rates*. The worst response rates typically are those associated with mail surveys. They also are not uncommon in telephone surveys carried out by inexperienced interviewing staffs or a staff of interviewers unused to accomplishing high response rates.

Generally speaking, a decision to carry out a survey without procedures to ensure a high rate of response is one of the worst design decisions that can be made. The self-selected portion of a sample that chooses to return a mail questionnaire is particularly problematic. Almost all studies of early returns of mail questionnaires show that they are a biased sample, biased in ways that are relevant directly to the subject matter of the survey. Hence the answers of such people are minority views and atypical of the population as a whole. The biases associated with low response rates to telephone surveys are somewhat less dramatic, although they consistently are likely to leave out the less educated and the elderly populations, groups likely to have distinctive views.

While there is no universal right answer in this respect, if response rates are going to drop below 70 percent, most researchers would have more accurate and useful estimates if they reduced their sample size and devoted the saved resources to obtaining responses from a higher percentage of the sample.

Because most people who think about survey design think about *sampling design*, very little time will be spent in this conclusion on that topic. If one is going to draw a sophisticated sample, the help of a qualified sampling statistician is needed. Presumably, such a statistician will consider tradeoffs among various sample schemes for the calculation of sampling errors. The one point that should be noted here is that the majority of population samples involve some clustering. In fact, multistage clustered samples are the best solution to a wide range of sampling problems. However, it is not uncommon to see reports in which the effects of clustering are ignored in estimates of sampling error. If researchers do not have an effective simple random sample, which is often the case, they cannot use simple random sampling assumptions in estimating standard errors.

The choice of *data collection mode* is one of the most fundamental choices affecting survey costs. While for years personal survey methods were considered the on.y effective way to carry out general population surveys, telephone strategies are now becoming more prevalent than personal interview surveys in most survey organizations.

For many purposes, the telephone has proved an effective way to produce survey data. However, a thorough accounting of the total cost of the telephone option does not always make it a best buy. Depending on the situation, telephone interviewing may be at a disadvantage in leaving out the segment of the population without telephones (the sample frame problem), in producing higher rates of nonresponse (although this is not always the case), and in permitting researchers to collect less data (since telephone interviews generally are designed to run shorter than personal interviews). Telephone survey procedures are the right answer for many projects. However, as for most cost-saving procedures, there are occasions when the nonmonetary price for choosing the telephone is too high.

The *quality of the interviewing staff* is probably one of the least appreciated aspects of survey research. Little credible research has been done on the amount of error that can be associated with the interviewer, but it recently has been shown that there are differences between well-trained and supervised interviewers and those who are less well trained. For a good number of common survey questions, poorly trained or supervised interviews can reduce the effective sample size by 20 or 30 percent. That means that a sample of 1000 may have the effective precision of a sample of only 700. Although the significance of interviewing quality varies with the content of the survey and the kinds of questions, most general purpose surveys will have at least some questions that will be affected significantly by interviewers. In this context, skimping on interviewer training and supervision may be a poor choice.

Another design decision related to interviewing has to do with the *number of interviews* that each interviewer takes. The effect of interviewers on data is exacerbated if assignment sizes are particularly large. For most studies, using more interviewers and not letting any individual interviewer take more than, say, 50 interviews is likely to be a cost-effective decision.

The quality of the interviewing staff also affects the response rate. Using a good interviewing staff that has proven it can achieve respondent cooperation is one of the easiest ways to ensure a good response rate. Close supervision, retraining, and the elimination of interviewers who are not good at enlisting cooperation are also steps that will pay off in reduced nonresponse and probably will not entail much extra cost.

We are just beginning to appreciate the potential of *better questionnaire design* for producing more reliable and valid measures. However, we know that asking several similar questions in different ways can produce better measures. Proper question design also has been shown to increase markedly the rate at which physician visits, health conditions, and hospitalizations are accurately reported (e.g., Cannell et al., 1977a).

Finally, the design of questionnaires also can reduce the extent to which interviewers affect answers. Standardized procedures that structure the way that interviewers relate to respondents can be built into questionnaires, further reducing the extent to which interviewers can be associated with the quality of reporting and improving the average level of respondent performance (Cannell et al., 1977b).

As discussed in the chapter on questionnaire design, there is still a good deal to be learned about how to use a questionnaire to maximize the quality of measurement. However, even at our current state of knowledge, for almost all surveys more investment in expert consultation and more extensive pretesting and pilot work would be relatively inexpensive steps to produce better survey-based estimates.

If only a few open-ended questions are included in a survey and the vast majority are closed questions, there is not a great deal of potential for error to be introduced into the data by the *coding* process. Also *verification of data entry and data cleaning* identify a very small number of errors, if the survey process has been designed in a professional way in other respects. On the other hand, the incremental costs of check coding, verification, and data cleaning tend to be modest in the context of total survey effort. In addition, if one is trying to make an estimate of a relatively rare event, a few coding or data reduction errors can make a difference of significance, and special care may pay off well in the quality of estimates.

CONCLUSION

The goals of good design and practice are to produce the most accuracy, credibility, and replicability possible for a dollar. How precise, credible, and replicable a particular study should be depends on the problem to be addressed and how the information will be used.

One will occasionally read that social science is inexact, and invidious comparisons are made between the measurement process in the social sciences and those in physical sciences. Although such conclusions are common, they commonly are uninformed. Basic measurements in physical and biomedical sciences, such as the level of lead in a blood sample, the readings of blood pressures, reading of X-rays, and the measures of the elasticity of metals all prove to have nontrivial levels of unreliability. Measurement in any of these fields can be made either better or worse by the methodology used and the care that goes into the design of the measurement process. Turner and Martin (1984) provide numerous examples. The same is true for survey research.

Virtually error-free measurement of many interesting characteristics of a population can be made using sample survey techniques. The problem is that the value of error-free measurement generally is not worth the cost. Sampling a population by sampling households omits people who cannot be associated with households. However, that is a very small fraction of the total population in most areas, and the cost of finding a way to sample people who cannot be associated with households is extraordinary.

Nonresponse rates can be reduced to virtually zero. The Public Health Service routinely achieves response rates in excess of 90 percent for its Health Interview Survey, though response rates are lower in central cities. If one wanted to spend enough time and money, one could probably achieve response rates close to 100 percent even in the most inhospitable segments of our most difficult central cities. However, again the cost would be extraordinary and the potential error reduction modest.

If one invests enough time and energy in training and supervision, one can get interviewers who perform to near perfection. However, again the trade-off in terms of cost and error reduction does not always justify going beyond a certain point.

Fortunately, respondents are able and willing to answer many questions of great interest to social scientists and policymakers. For some other questions it would be convenient if respondents were able and willing to answer in a standard survey process, but they are not. For example, drunk driving convictions and bankruptcies markedly are underreported using standard survey techniques (Locander et al., 1976). There probably is some way that a research project could be presented that would induce most people to report such facts accurately, but it would take a great deal more effort than researchers generally make to gain respondent cooperation. Again there are decisions to be made about how much accuracy and detail are worth in the context of how the data will be used.

It has been said that the limit of survey research is what people are able and willing to tell us in the context of the survey. However, those limits can be stretched. There certainly are some real limits to what can be measured accurately using standardized survey procedures. However, the limits probably are related much more often to budgetary considerations and how much effort the researcher wants to put into the measurement process than related to what is actually feasible.

So error in survey estimates exists more because it is acceptable than because it is unavoidable. The context in which one evaluates a design is whether or not the compromises made were the right ones, the intelligent ones, and the ones that would produce data appropriate to the purposes at hand. It also is worth pointing out that survey error does not result solely from thoughtful, cost-saving decisions. There also has not been adequate appreciation of the significance of nonresponse, questionnaire design, and interviewer performance for the quality of survey estimates. Sheer lack of attention to these important aspects of data collection routinely produces survey data that lack credibility or do not meet state-of-the-art standards for reliability (see, for example, Bailar & Lanphier, 1978; Turner & Martin, 1984).

Appreciating the concept of total design promulgated in this book should mean that:

(1) No feature of a data collection will be so poor or so weak that it would undermine the researcher's ability to use the data for the purpose at hand.
(2) The design of all phases of the data collection will be relatively consistent, so that investments are not made in producing precision in one aspect of the data collection process that are not justified by the level of precision that other aspects of the design will generate.
(3) Users of survey data will have an appropriate respect both for the uses of the estimates based on a sample survey, the likely sources of error in surveys, and the limits in accuracy and confidence that they can have in survey-based estimates.

Finally, it is hoped that users of research will have a thorough grasp of the questions they should ask about the data collection in any survey, that researchers have a better grasp of the significance of the details of their design decisions, and that all readers come away with a renewed commitment to better survey design and execution.

REFERENCES

Bailar, Barbara A. & Lanphier, C. M. (1978). *Development of survey research methods to assess survey practices*. Washington: American Statistical Association.

Belson, William A. (1981). *The design and understanding of survey questions*. Aldershot, England: Gower.

Bradburn, N. A., Sudman, S. & associates (1979). *Improving interview methods and questionnaire design*. San Francisco: Jossey-Bass.

Bryson, M. C. (1976). The literary digest poll: Making of a statistical myth. *American Statistician*, November, 184-185.

Cannell, C. F., & Fowler, F. J., Jr. (1964). A note on interviewer effect in self-enumerative procedures. *American Sociological Review, 29,*276.

Cannell, C. F. & Fowler, F. J. (1965). "Comparison of hospitalization reporting in three survey procedures." *In Vital and health statistics*, Series 2, No. 8. Washington, DC: U.S. Government Printing Office.

Cannell, C. F., Lawson, S. A., & Hansen, D. L. (1975), *A technique for evaluating interviewer performance*. Ann Arbor: Institute for Social Research.

Cannell, C. F., Marquis, K. H. & Laurent, A. (1977a). "A summary of studies." *Vital and health statistics*, Series, 2, 69. Washington, DC: U.S. Government Printing Offfice.

Cannell, C. F., Oksenberg, L., & Converse, J. M. (1977b). *Experiments in interviewing techniques: Field experiments in health reporting: 1971-1977*. Hyattsville M D : NCHSR.

Colombotos, J. (1969). Personal versus telephone interviews: effect on responses. *Public Health Reports, 84* 773-782.

Cronbach, L. J. (1951). Coefficient alpha and the internal structure of tests. *Psychatrika, 16* 297-334.

Cronbach, L. J., & Meehl, P. E. (1955). Construct validity in psychological tests. *Psychological Bulletin, 52,* 281-302.

DeMaio, T. J. (Ed.) (1983). *Approaches to developing questionnaires*. Statistical Policy Working Paper 10. Washington, DC: U.S. Government Printing Office.

Densen, P., Shapiro, S., & Balamuth, E. (1963). "Health interview responses compared with medical records." *Vital and Health Statistics*, Series 2, 7. Washington, DC: U.S. Government Printing Office.

Dillman, D.A. (1978). *Mail and telephone surveys: The total design method*. New York: John Wiley.

Dillman, D. A., Carpenter, E., Christensen, J., & Brooks, R. (1974). "Increasing mail questionnaire response: a four state comparison." *American Sociological Review, 39,* 5, 744-756.

Donald, M. N. (1960). Implications of nonresponse for the interpretation of mail questionnaire data. *Public Opinion Quarterly, 24,* 99-114.

Erlich, J. & Riesman, D. (1961). Age and authority in the intrview. *Public Opinion Quarterly, 25,* 39-56.

Fowler, F. J. (1966). *Education, interaction and interview performance*. Doctoral dissertation, University of Michigan.

Fowler, F. J., Jr., & Mangione, T. W. (1983). The role of interviewing training and supervision in reducing interviewer effects on survey data. *Proceedings of the American Statistical Association Meeting*, Survey Reseach Methods Section, 124-128.

Friedman, P. A. (1942). A second experiment in interviewer bias. *Sociometry, 15,* 378-381.

Greenberg, B. G., Abdel-Latif, A. A., Simmons, W. R., & Horvitz, D. (1969). The unrelated question randomized response model: theoretical framework. *Journal of the American Statistical Association, 64*, 326, 520-539.

Groves, R. M., & Kahn, R. L. (1979). *Surveys by telephone: A national comparison with personal interviews*, New York: Academic Press.

Groves, R. M., & Magilavy, L. J. (1980). Estimates of interviewer variance in telephone surveys. *Proceedings of the American Statistical Association*, Survey Research Methods Section, 622-627.

Guenzel, P. J., Berkmans, T. R., & Cannell, C. F. (1983). *General interviewing techniques.* Ann Arbor: Institute for Social Research.

Hanson, R. H., & Marks, E. S. (1958). Influence of the interviewer on the accuracy of survey results. *Journal of the American Statistical Association, 53*, 635-655.

Hensen, R., Roth, A., & Cannell, C. (1977). Personal versus telephone interviews: the effects of telephone reinterviews on reporting of psychiatric symptomatology. In C. F. Cannell et al., *Experiments in interviewing techniques: Field experiments in health reporting, 1971-1977* (pp. 205-219). Hyattsville: NCHSR.

Hochstim, J. R. (1967). A critical comparison of three strategies of collecting data from households. *Journal of the American Statistical Association, 62*, September, 976-989.

Hyman, H. H., Cobb, J., Feldman, J., & Stember, C. (1954). *Interviewing in social research.* Chicago: University of Chicago Press.

Kahn, R., & Cannell, C. F. (1958). *Dynamics of interviewing.* New York: John Wiley.

Kalton, G. (1983). *Introduction to survey sampling.* Beverly Hills, CA: Sage Publications.

Katz, E. (1942). Do interviewers bias poll results? *Public Opinion Quarterly, 6*, 248-268.

Kinsey, A. C., Pomeroy, W. B., & Martin, C. E. (1948). *Sexual behavior in the human male.* Philadelphia: W. B. Sanders.

Kish, L. (1949). A procedure for objective respondent selection within the household. *Journal of the American Statistical Association, 44*, 380-387.

Kish, L. (1962). Studies of interviewer variance for attitudinal variables. *Journal of the American Statistical Association, 57*, 92-115.

Klecka, W. R., & Tuchfarber, A. J. (1978). Random digit dialing: a comparison of personal surveys. *Public Opinion Quarterly, 42*, 105-114.

Likert, R. (1932). A technique for measurement of attitudes. *Arch. Psychology, 140*.

Linsky, A. (1975). Stimulating response to mailed questionnaires: A review. *Public Opinion Quarterly, 39*, 82-101.

Locander, W., Sudman, S., & Bradburn, N. (1976). An investigation of interview method, threat and response distortion. *Journal of the American Statistical Association, 71*, 354, 269-275.

Madow, W. C. (1963). "Interview data on chronic conditions compared with information derived from medical records." *Vital and Health Statistics*, Series 2, 23. Washington, DC: U.S. Government Printing Office.

Mangione, T. W., Hingson, R., & Barrett, J. (1982). Collecting sensitive data: a comparison of three survey strategies. *Sociological Methods and Research, 10*, 3, 337-346.

Marquis, K. H. (1978). Survey response rates: some trends, causes, and correlates. In *U.S. National Center for Health Services Research*, Health Survey Research Methods: Second Biennial Conference, 1977, pp. 3-12. DHEW Pub. No. (PHS) 79-3207. Hyattsville, MD: NCHSR.

Marquis, K. H., & Cannell, C. F. (1971). "Effect of some experimental interviewing techniques on reporting in the health interview study." *Vital and Health Statistics*, Series 2, No. 41. Washington, DC: U.S. Government Printing Office.

Marquis, K. H., Cannell, C. F., & Laurent, A. (1972). "Reporting for health events in household interviews: effects of reinforcement, question length, and reinterviews." *Vital and Health Statistics*, Series 2, No. 45. Washington, DC: U.S. Government Printing Office.

NCHSR. (1977). *Advances in health survey research methods*. Washington, DC: U.S. Public Service.

Payne, S. L. (1951). *The art of asking questions*. Princeton, NJ: Princeton University Press.

Robinson, D., & Rohde, S. (1946). Two experiments with an anti-Semitism poll. *Journal of Abnormal Social Psychology, 41,* 136-144.

Schuman, H., & Converse, J. M. (1971). Effects of black and white interviewers on black responses in 1968. *The Public Opinion Quarterly, 35,* 1, 44-68.

Schuman, H., & Presser, S. (1981). *Questions and answers in attitude surveys*. New York: Academic Press.

Singer, E. (1981). Telephone interviewing and black box. In *Health Survey Research Methods*, Third Biennial Conference, pp. 124-127. Washington, DC: National Center for Health Services Research.

Sudman, S. (1967). *Reducing the cost of surveys*. Chicago: Aldine.

Sudman, S. (1976). *Applied sampling*. New York: Academic Press.

Sudman, S., & Bradburn, N. M. (1974). *Response effects in surveys: A review and synthesis*. Chicago: Aldine.

Sudman, S., & Bradburn, N. M. (1982). *Asking questions*. San Francisco: Jossey-Bass.

Sudman, S. et al. (1974). *The cost-effectiveness of using the diary*. Urbana: University of Illinois Research Laboratory.

Thurstone, L. L. & Chave, E. J. (1929). *The measurement of attitude*. Chicago: University of Chicago.

Turner, C. S., & Martin, E. (Eds.). (1984). *Surveying subjective phenomena*. New York: Russell Sage Foundation.

Waksberg, J. (1978). Sampling methods for random digit dialing. *Journal of the American Statistical Association, 73,* 40-66.

Weiss, C. H. (1968). Validity of welfare mothers' interview responses. *Public Opinion Quarterly, 32,* 4, 622-633.

INDEX

ABOUT THE AUTHOR

Floyd J. Fowler, Jr., received a Ph.D. in social psychology from the University of Michigan in 1966. While there, he got his first taste of methodological research, working on several studies of the sources of error in the National Health Interview Survey.

Since then Dr. Fowler has devoted his professional career to learning about, improving, and applying survey methodology. He has been principal investigator for major survey studies of local population trends, attitudes toward local government and services, gambling law enforcement, racial tensions, fear of crime, Jewish identification, and the needs of the elderly. He has provided methodological assistance on well over 100 survey projects, covering most of the substantive policy areas to which survey research is applied. He has taught survey research methods at the Harvard School of Public Health and elsewhere. For 12 years, he was Director of the Center for Survey Research, a facility of the University of Massachusetts, Boston, and the Joint Center for Urban Studies of MIT and Harvard University. He is currently a Senior Research Fellow at the Center.

DATE DUE

~~APR 27 1990~~			
6/10/99	ILL # 1006726		

DEMCO 38-297